Becoming Soulmates

HOW TO SHARE A DEEPLY PASSIONATE JOURNEY WHERE CHALLENGES STRENGTHEN LOVE

BY JOHN GREY, PH.D. AND BONNEY GREY, R.N.

LEAP FROG PRESS

DEDICATED TO ASIA

AND TO ALL SEEKERS OF HIGH-QUALITY
CONSCIOUS RELATIONSHIPS

BECOMING SOULMATES

Copyright © 2001 by John Grey and Bonney Grey.

For information write:

LEAP FROG PRESS
501 Swain Avenue, Sebastopol, CA 95472

email: lovegrowth@aol.com
website : www.soulmateoracle.com

The authors coach singles and couples throughout the country by phone. They also present workshops on conscious loving. And they offer a unique weekend retreat for couples to clarify and transform their relationships.

Information about these coaching services—as well as self-help tools—can be found on the internet at:

www. soulmateoracle. com

You can also contact the authors by email at:

lovegrowth@aol.com

CONTENTS

PREFACE

In our work as relationship counselors, we know many couples start out having magical, open-hearted feelings where each senses they've found their soulmate—someone with whom they deeply desire to have a lasting relationship.

Given such a strong start, one wonders how anything could ever possibly go wrong. But as we all know, the magic doesn't last forever and "happily ever after" also involves some serious challenges along the way.

This is the part they don't show at the movies.

Our movies, songs, fairy tales and myths of the perfect love focus entirely on the bliss of the honeymoon. We can end up thinking that the "right" person—by definition—is someone who never upsets us, someone who always makes us feel good. It's just like magic!

In fact, for most people, the sense of magic ends the day that problems, differences or upsetting issues appear. As counselors, we've seen many *potential* soulmates get lost in problems. They wonder if they are truly with the right other person, because they are feeling upset instead of joyful.

The popular myths of love do not educates us about what to do with upsets or differences. Oh sure, we have heard that "relationships require work." But what exactly *is* that work? Chances are, most of us have never seen a couple deal with upset in a way that strengthened their love.

When the two of us first got together as a couple, we had been counselors for a decade. Yet even we still had not seen any great models of healthy soulmates in the real world. We still had in front of us the task of learning what it would take to turn the flame that our love ignited into a lasting relationship, rather than just another burning house.

So when the magic of our honeymoon period subsided, we had a strong urge to do things differently this time around, to make this love work, to learn to be soulmates.

We found that to progress together and deepen our love, we had to throw out a lot of old ways of thinking and forge a new path. That path has changed us for the better. And it changed the way we counsel others as well.

In this book we want to point to the depth of love that is indeed possible to share in this lifetime. And we want to show you how becoming soulmates is a process—not just a matter of finding the perfect person.

The intent of this book is to help you understand the inner workings of that process—and to provide you with the tools for creating the quality of love you truly want to share with another person in your life.

John & Bonney Grey
Sebastopol, California
February 2, 2000

CHAPTER ONE

LOVE STARTS LIKE AN ADVENTURE

"Blessed is the influence of one true,
loving human soul on another."
—GEORGE ELIOT

The deep yearning to share life with someone moves most of us toward relationship. Our hearts dream of a union that will add sparkle to the experience of being.

When we fall in love, we find bliss and inspiration. It can be like sailing to a tropical island paradise. We are exploring new territory—the magnificently unfamiliar. We are in the honeymoon of a new beginning.

- Open
- Exciting
- Sharing
- Adventurous
- Curious
- Unfamiliar

The honeymoon is a time of magic and wonder. We feel fresh and alive—charged with excitement, curiosity and new possibility. We want to share every possible moment with our new found lover.

Hearts open. Spirits soar. The sun is shining brightly. We are filled with hope. We are undeniably altered, transcendent and expansive.

We may feel we found our true soulmate!

Some say the honeymoon is like a spiritual experience.

Others—perhaps those not currently under its spell—claim it's an alteration in brain chemistry, a state of temporary intoxication, a delusion that will pass with time.

Since our theme is soulmates, let's explore the analogy that the honeymoon is like a spiritual experience. We are talking not of any specific religion, but of that which touches us with an indefinably great energy that lifts our souls.

Spiritual experiences can spontaneously arise from things like a arriving at the coast and seeing a breathtaking sunset; being swept away in a concert of great music; or experiencing the profound quite of a peaceful forest. These are moments of inspiration that fall on us like divine gifts from the sky.

When we are truly touched by spiritual experience, our souls are uplifted. We rise above the fixations of daily life. It expands our hearts and minds. We may get a greater sense of meaning for our lives. We may be inspired to face difficulties and challenges in a more positive light.

When we fall deeply in love, our souls similarly expand. The uplift can match the purest spiritual experience.

The honeymoon opens us. We feel we've encountered the divine. In this phase of love, in this expansion of our souls, we may feel we have met our soulmate.

WHAT IS A SOULMATE?

Popular definitions of "soulmates" and "true love" tend to focus on the elated feelings found in the honeymoon of a new relationship. Movies show it—songs sing it loudly.

The popular idea goes something like this:

"A soulmate is that special someone who uplifts and expands my soul!"

Poetic embellishments of the definition of a soulmate and true love go all the way back to Elizabethan times:

> *"I'll be as patient as a gentle stream,*
> *And make a pastime of each weary step,*
> *Till the last step have brought me to my love;*
> *And there I'll rest, as after much turmoil*
> *A blessed soul doth in Elysium."*
> —SHAKESPEARE

ANOTHER PHASE OF LOVE

Unfortunately, the honeymoon does not last indefinitely. There is another phase of relating that soon follows. This is a part Hollywood seldom shows. It's the theme of mournful love songs. It starts when the honeymoon is over.

"The honeymoon is over!"

We've talked to people who report they already met their soulmate—then lost them. The pain buried in such a loss seems to linger for years, even decades.

We hear this from singles still mourning a lost love which is unmatched by anything since. Other reports are made by people in a relationship, where the quality of their love has shifted downward. Instead of being uplifted, they now feel their mate lowers their spirits.

We frequently hear people say, "I was convinced that this person was my true soulmate. Those feelings were real... And I still feel the loss."

How can we explain this? After all, isn't a soulmate that one, special person we will meet, marry and be happy with for the rest of our lives? You know, the "they lived happily ever after" ending to the movie.

How could we find such a special person—our true love— and then lose them so easily?

Look closely at the assumptions expressed above. Let's scrutinize the popular myth of "true love." How does it apply it to the actualities of love in the real world? Does the myth stack up to the reality of your actual experience?

Consider the popular assumptions about a what true love

and a perfect relationship is:

• "There is one right person in the world for you—one perfect partner—one soulmate."
• "With your soulmate, you'll live happily ever after."
• "With your soulmate, you'll always feel uplifted."
• "To feel unhappy is undesirable—the very opposite of what a perfect relationship should be about."
• "If you stop feeling uplifted, it's a bad sign."
• "If a lot of upsets or difficulties arise, you'd have reason to doubt you are in the right relationship at all."

DOUBT IN THE TEMPLE OF LOVE

Our popular myth of "true love" is largely focused on the expansive feelings of the honeymoon. So, if unhappy feelings arise, we may begin to doubt a relationship.

In some cases, this doubt may well be appropriate. Yet in many situations, it may be hiding our own need to grow and develop new skills as individuals. If we had those skills, maybe we could create the relationship we truly want.

Let's return to our metaphor that the honeymoon is like a spiritual experience.

Contrast a spiritual experience... with a spiritual practice.

A spiritual *experience* is often spontaneous. It's a gift. We open to receive it. We are in a receptive role.

A spiritual *practice*, on the other hand, usually asks us to get involved in an active process. This may include activities that tap into our own power to expand our souls—such as meditation or prayer.

In love, at least in the honeymoon, we are in a receptive role. We are suddenly and unexpectedly expanded—seemingly by something, or someone, outside of us. During this phase, we may feel our partner embodies our inspiration, that they are the factor that is lifting and expanding our soul.

Yet when differences or upsets arise in our relationship, we may find ourselves without an outside source of inspiration. At these times, both partners may be looking for that missing uplift from one another—and yet neither is able to deliver much inspiration.

This is the moment when a couple turns from the bliss of a honeymoon to the sadness of missing it. Disappointment sets in. Each may begin to resent the fact that their soul is no longer being lifted up and inspired by the other.

In writing a guidebook to a lasting relationship, we aim higher than offering tools to help a relationship merely persist through time. Far too many marriages drag on through decades of unhappiness and dissatisfaction.

Our aim is to help you move beyond a receptive role in relationship—where your are trapped into being *reactive.*

We aim to show you a place of power, of being *proactive.*

Being reactive may lead you to great highs as well as deep lows. You may be inspired by meeting a new love. That's a reaction to something on the outside. Then sometime later, you may be devastated by something they do—or by something they don't do. Again, a reaction to something on the outside.

Where are *you* in that equation? Read on.

BEING PROACTIVE

Let's return for a moment more to the analogy of spiritual experiences and spiritual practices.

Spiritual practices encourage us to take an active role in the evolution of our souls. While we can remain in a receptive role and occasionally have great spiritual experiences, we may not fully evolve ourselves if we never take an active part in our own growth.

This means being proactive, showing up consciously.

It is similar in love. At first we coast along unconsciously in a purely receptive role. All we have to do is open to all those great spontaneous honeymoon feelings.

But in the next phase of love—beyond the honeymoon—we are called upon to show up in a conscious, more proactive way. In love, we can't remain in the receptive role and hope to continually be uplifted. Something needs to shift.

After the honeymoon—in real-world relationships—we will sometimes get upset, and draw each other into that upset.

Then who is left to deliver the inspiration?

Nobody!

Seduced by the receptive phase of love and by the popular myths of "true love"—we unconsciously define our perfect parter as someone who uplifts us even when we are down.

So when the honeymoon is over, our feeling of being with our soulmate may also be put into doubt.

Perhaps you have already noticed that the popular myth of "soulmate" leaves out that old saying: "A good relationship takes work!"

This is not an insignificant omission.

Indeed, if we want turn the honeymoon into a lasting relationship, we need to bring it down to earth. We need to revise our own personal definition of true love to recognize that "ever after" includes feelings other than happiness.

There will be challenges and we will be required to do work. As the honeymoon ends, we shift out of the purely receptive phase of love. We enter the next phase, which asks us to be conscious, to proactively show up in a new way.

Relationships are our greatest teacher. They tell us what we need to learn next in life to grow as individuals. We are called upon to expand our souls, heal our past wounds and evolve as humans.

Love is that which brings up our lesson plan. Doing the "work" of relationship goes far beyond simply learning to communicate better. We will give you important tools to improve communication in this book.

However, we aim higher yet. We have found the work that results in a lasting and satisfying relationship with a soulmate will involve you in your own inner personal growth.

This is the deeper substance of this book. It will give you tools to be on a conscious journey of your own making, a co-explorer of a new path with your soulmate.

This will mean you showing up in a new way when both of you get stuck in upset or negativity. It means embracing the upsets and learning how to expand and elevate the situation.

In the work of relationship, when the honeymoon's over you are called on to instigate positive transformation. You are asked to co-create and take a new path with your partner.

Each partner needs to come forward in times of challenge and expand to the occasion, rather than closing down. The main thing that prevents us from doing this work is the lack of a good model for how to do it.

We are sadly lacking in useful guidelines for doing the work of relationship. We have few understandings that lift us to transform, much less resolve, our upsets.

Most of us were raised in families which did not model how to positively resolve the challenges in relationship. We have seldom seen it done well, and may not even know a couple that can do it.

On the contrary, we mostly see and talk about couples who are stuck in drama or unhappiness. We know couples who are doing a lot of work—that does not work!

Because of the abysmal state of love and relationship that runs throughout our society, it is becoming clear that we need to learn to do a new kind of relationship work. Let's start this now, and forge our own definition of "soulmate."

How do you know when you are truly with your soulmate?

It's not a matter of magic feelings. It's very simple:

You know you're with your soulmate when you are both consciously doing your personal growth in the relationship.

This means that you can only find out if you're with a soulmate by going through times of challenge or upset. You cannot gauge it by the honeymoon phase alone.

To know if you are with a true soulmate, you need to see

how you both show up and consciously "work" with upsets, sensitivities, differences and challenges.

Unfortunately, many potential soulmates get lost because they don't know how to do relationship work. They hold onto the popular unconscious myth of "true love"—where upset feelings shouldn't happen, where upset is a bad sign.

Or couples may work real hard, but like talking a problem in circles, they exhaust their hearts in ineffective unconscious strategies—until they finally give up or split up.

Many people feel they have met a soulmate, but then, somehow, lost them. One man at a lecture we gave sadly said, "I was with my soulmate ten years ago. I just don't know what happened. I can't get her out of my mind."

At the end of the talk, after we had presented the basic principles in this book, he said, "I realize now that I just did not have effective, conscious skills to work with our problems. I wish I'd heard this talk a decade ago."

Something clicked for him. He realized that the future held the possibility of another love, and that it was crucial for him to consciously commit to his personal growth now.

LOVE & PERSONAL GROWTH

The growth work in becoming soulmates is the subject of this book. We offer you skills and understandings that will help you to create and sustain a deeply satisfying, profoundly meaningful and lasting relationship—provided you are willing to grow as an individual.

Ultimately, the quality of relationship you can have is directly linked to your willingness to engage in personal growth. It is linked to how willing you are to expand your mind and heart. And it is linked to how proactive you are in creating the love you want.

We live in a time that needs new models for relationship. The divorce rate remains high, decade after decade. Half of marriages end in pain. Certainly few of them began that way. A large percentage of divorced couples report deep regrets that they didn't know how to work things out.

Any work they tried to do—absolutely did *not* work!

Research is showing us interesting facts. Couples who stay together have as many issues as couples who split up. The difference is not the absence of conflict, but the skills they bring to the table to work with the challenges that come up.

Skills can be learned. Quality relating is not some abstract or unobtainable thing. Nor is it a matter of luck.

We need to revise our models of love and relating in a way that helps us face the challenges and see these as pathways to strengthen our love.

Challenges help us grow, as individuals and as couples.

There's a story[1] about a group of kids who go for a walk and discover a cocoon. Fascinated, they gather and watch as the butterfly inside works hard to get free. A girl in the group suggests they time the event. As the butterfly stretches and struggles, it pushes out of the cocoon, little by little.

The children groan with each push. Eventually, after an agonizing fifteen minutes, the butterfly breaks free and spreads its colorful wings in flight.

As the children continue to walk, they soon find a second cocoon. It also is in a state of excited movement. Having witnessed the first, one child sympathetically asks how they

might help this second butterfly get free, faster.

"Why should it work so much?"

They agree. A boy takes out his pocketknife and gently makes a slit in the cocoon. Sure enough, the butterfly is able to flop out with little struggle, in less than two minutes!

But quickly it begins to contract and close up on itself. Within minutes it is dead.

Shocked, they later talk to their teacher, who reveals an important fact. The butterfly, in stretching and pushing inside the cocoon, is moving fluids into veinlike structures in its wings that strengthen its frame. The struggle is what allows the butterfly to complete its transformation from caterpillar to a magnificent flying creature. Only by fully engaging in the challenges of the cocoon can the butterfly ever spread its wings in flight.

So too, must we fully engage in the challenges that arise in love to actualize our true soulmate potential. In this spirit, we begin our journey.

CHAPTER TWO

BEYOND THE HONEYMOON

"The course of true love never did run smooth."
— SHAKESPEARE

We all know that sooner or later the honeymoon is over. It may last weeks, months, or even years. But it does end at some point. And then another phase of relationship begins....

WHAT HAPPENS WHEN
"The honeymoon is over!"

What happens? A return to reality? Is "real life" finally entering the equation? Does perfect love somehow just slip away? Sadly, many of us may look back at our honeymoon period only to feel we lost something, the rest of our lives together never quite measuring up to it.

The honeymoon gives us a glimpse of possibility for a relationship. This book shows how couples can make good on that possibility and turn it into a lasting reality. It offers a model, and a pathway to becoming deeper soulmates.

The first step on this path is to understand what happens when the honeymoon ends. This is a critical moment in a relationship. How you respond makes a big difference.

What signals the crossing of this dreaded threshold? What exactly are the signs?

SIGNS THAT THE HONEYMOON IS OVER

- **Problems**
- **Challenges**
- **Upsets**
- **Differences**

Conventional Wisdom: These are all seen as negative signs.

Couples usually declare the honeymoon is over when *problems, challenges, upsets* or *differences* arise.

These are normally seen as negative signs—signs that something is "wrong"—signs of a "bad" relationship.

Most couples will look for the "cause" of these unwanted events. Inevitably, they point the finger at each other. Getting the other person to change is seen as the way back to the wonderful spontaneous feelings of the honeymoon.

This is not a conscious strategy. It is a knee-jerk reaction. Seeing a problem, challenge, upset or differences as a negative sign is the normal thing to do, the conventional wisdom. But it is not the wisdom of longlasting soulmates.

It is rare to find people who greet problems by saying "Wow, this is great! More excitement and fun!" Soulmates may not say that, either. But they do greet challenges with a different mindset. They do not necessarily see challenges or upsets as unwanted negative signs.

Unconsciously, most of us *do* see things according to the conventional wisdom. We may feel that "differences attract" at first meeting. But after the honeymoon, people normally start to complain about how "unlike me" the other person is. There's a tendency to see the other person as "wrong" or deficient in character, because they are different.

How does this happen? Let's look at the underlying process that turns problems, upsets and differences into road blocks to happiness.

VICIOUS CIRCLE

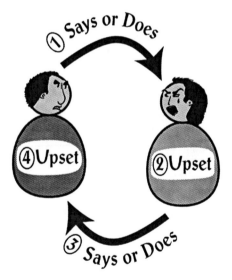

We call it the Vicious Circle. It starts when (1) a person says or does something, and (2) the other person gets upset. Then (3) that person says or does something in return, and (4) the first person gets upset. Continuing around the circle, (1) they repeat the process.

The couple is off and running. Around and around the circle they go. In a matter of minutes emotions can heat. It can take days or weeks to recover.

Here's an example. This was the defining moment when Sarah and Michael knew their honeymoon was over. They were driving to a meeting that was going to challenge her. She was unusually quiet and inward.

Noticing this, Michael wanted to lighten things up and relieve the tension. He tried to inject a little humor the way he normally did with his friends, by lightly teasing her. Sarah remained quiet, so he continued to try to draw her out by teasing. Suddenly, she blew up and called him insensitive.

Michael reacted with sarcasm, which was not received any better than the teasing had been. He said she was ruining the trip and blamed her for not responding to his good intentions like his friends would have.

This gave evidence to the old saying that the road to the Hole is paved with good intentions.

Only minutes had passed and they were going around the Vicious Circle with increasing speed. This was their first fight. They stayed upset over it for a week.

The Vicious Circle can quickly turn into a Downward Spiral, and it leads to the "Hole." As this happens, there are a number of things that couples, not acting like soulmates, typically say or do.

You may hear one person blaming the other for causing the situation. Like, "You make me angry!"

You may hear name calling. One person calls the other "insensitive" or "selfish" or some other negative label.

There are classic red-flag words — "always," "never,"

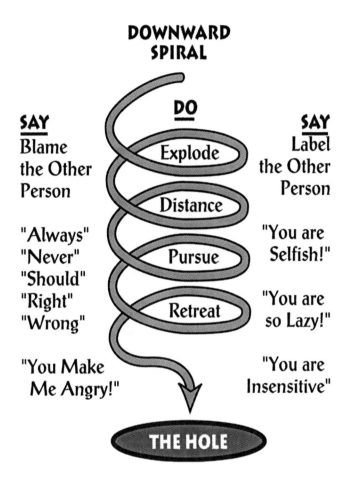

DOWNWARD SPIRAL

DO

SAY
Blame
the Other
Person

"Always"
"Never"
"Should"
"Right"
"Wrong"

"You Make
Me Angry!"

Explode

Distance

Pursue

Retreat

SAY
Label
the Other
Person

"You are
Selfish!"

"You are
so Lazy!"

"You are
Insensitive"

THE HOLE

"should," "right" and "wrong"—words that reveal that the mind is narrowing or getting lost in judgments.

Behind such words, the emotional arena has collapsed into a basic reaction of "fight or flight." There may be anger or pursuit, distancing or retreat. Depending upon the couple, things can get explosive—or stone cold.

Couples in the Hole are dominated by their reactivity. The

"fight or flight" reaction powerfully alters body-brain chemistry. It's the chemistry that ancient humans needed to battle or escape a tiger suddenly appearing in the jungle.

In relationship, this chemical reaction fundamentally changes how we talk and act. It is like being very intoxicated. Very very intoxicated. The chemicals have taken over.

This is important to realize. When you are in the Hole— you are *under the influence*. As the brain's chemical balance shifts in preparation for "fight or flight," our pulse rate and breathing alters, our perception narrows, and our mental capacity collapses into black and white thinking.

Statements get dramatized and overgeneralized. You hear things like, "You *never* help me around here!" "I'm *always* cleaning up after you!"

In the Hole, our positive options are sharply reduced—if not gone altogether. Yet, people keep trying to resolve the situation, as if they could! Each wants to put in the final word. Emotions escalate. Someone may explode or leave.

Most couples can recognize their own version of being in the Hole. One question we have repeatedly asked is:

"Has there ever been one time when you were in the Hole and able to work things out in a successful way?"

We have yet to hear a single story of any such success.

Nor are we likely to, for a very good reason: solving an interpersonal issue takes skill.

Would you do brain surgery if you were totally drunk? Then why try to negotiate an important issue when you are under the influence of the chemistry of "fight or flight"?

Soulmates do not try to solve things if they fall into the Hole. In fact, they avoid the Hole as much as possible.

No matter how hard you might try to "work" on things, if you're in the Hole, you can only make matters worse. This is "work" that absolutely *does not work*. The strategies you use in the Hole are what *destroy* a relationship.

IN THE HOLE YOU ONLY DESTROY LOVE

- Blame the other person
- Label the other person
- Criticize the other person
- See them as the cause of your feelings
- Be defensive
- Stonewall, shut down & distance
- Win-Lose, "right" vs. "wrong"

BLAME: "You ruined our entire vacation!"
LABEL: "You are weak!" "You're such a slob!"
CRITICIZE: "You're self-centered!" "You are needy!"
CAUSE: "You frustrate me!" "You make me upset!"
DEFENSIVE: "That's your problem!"
　　　　　　"What about when you..."
STONEWALL: Walk out. Avoid the issue.
WIN-LOSE: "You're wrong!" "You never do it right."

Most of us can recognize one or more of these strategies. They seem like normal things to do when you are upset. But be warned. They can damage love beyond repair.

Unless you develop different strategies to resolve issues, the strategies of the Hole will either destroy your partnership, or leave you sharing long term unhappiness.

Wise soulmates avoid these strategies like the plague.

In our practice, when we first see couples we often hear reports from the Hole. Each partner makes a case for how they are right, how the other person needs to change.

We ask them, "Would you rather be right—or happy?"

Contrast the strategies of the Hole with the ones below, which *are* effective in solving interpersonal issues. These are keys for building long-term happiness in love.

Wise soulmates only attempt to resolve issues when they are clearly outside of the Hole. If they find themselves moving toward the Hole, they will stop and continue later when they can be more resourceful.

Later in this book, you will learn a clear and simple way to avoid falling into the Hole and being under its destructive influence.

But now let us look closely at how the items on the list below differ from the strategies of the Hole:

OUTSIDE THE HOLE YOU RESOLVE ISSUES

- Be curious about the other person
- See your own part in things
- Own and self-care for your feelings
- Listen to the other's viewpoint
- Open to hear what's true for them
- Consider their sensitivities
- Win-Win, mutual solutions

BE CURIOUS ABOUT THE OTHER PERSON. Instead of trying to LABEL or CRITICIZE your partner, you become *curious* about what is happening inside of them. Suspending your own judgments, you ask them what is going on for them. You then will learn something new about them, and they won't feel under attack.

SEE YOUR OWN PART IN THINGS. Instead of putting the BLAME on them for the situation, you *see your own part* in how things developed. This gives you an active role in changing things, and empowers you to avoid similar traps in the future.

OWN AND SELF-CARE FOR YOUR FEELINGS. Instead of making them the CAUSE of what you feel, you *own* your feelings. Instead of needing them to change in order to fix how you feel, you begin to learn to *self-care* for and heal your emotional states.

LISTEN TO THE OTHER'S VIEWPOINT. Instead of getting DEFENSIVE over what your partner may be saying, you *listen.* You get to understand their viewpoint and learn more about their sensitivities. This helps you avoid hot buttons in the future.

OPEN TO HEAR WHAT'S TRUE FOR THEM. Instead of starting to STONEWALL or CLOSE DOWN, you *open* to hear what is true for your partner. They feel heard, understood and accepted as human beings. This is a basic requirement for a relationship to grow and prosper.

CONSIDER THEIR SENSITIVITIES. Instead of being exclusively focused on your own needs and feelings, you can also consider the other person's sensitivities, as well. Partners who work things out together well have developed a map of each other's hot buttons and sensitivities. They know how to avoid setting off emotional landmines.

WIN-WIN MUTUAL SOLUTION. Instead of a WIN-LOSE outcome, you are interested in finding a *mutually* satisfactory solution. You will take into account the other person's needs. This enables you to co-create happiness together on an ongoing and lasting basis.

Unfortunately, a majority of us have not been exposed to many positive strategies for dealing with issues from outside the Hole. We probably did not see many of these constructive ways of relating when we were growing up.

This is one reason that today there are a lot of unhappy couples who mainly deal with issues from inside of the Hole. Until we consciously learn to do something different, we just repeat the relationship strategies we saw or developed in our childhood. How many of us had the good fortune to be shown constructive relating skills early in life? Consider the lucky child in the following story[2]:

There was once a small boy who found a green turtle. He started to examine it but then the turtle pulled in its head and closed its shell tight like a vice. The boy was upset, so he picked up a stick to try to pry it open.

The boy's father saw this and remarked, "No, son, that's not the way! In fact, you may poke at it—and even kill the turtle—but you'll never get it to open up with a stick."

His father took the turtle indoors and set it near the fireplace. It wasn't but a few minutes until it began to get warm. Then the turtle pushed out its head, stretched out its legs and began to crawl.

"Turtles are like that," said the father, "and people, too. You can't force them into anything by poking at them. But if you first warm them up with some real kindness, more than likely, they will open and come out of their shell."

What a lucky child to be taught an important lesson: use skillful relating instead of poking or using force. Otherwise people close up and get defensive.

So what if we didn't get taught such positive lessons in childhood—by word or example? This only means that we have to learn them now.

The good news is that these new skills *can* be learned.

Curiosity is a powerful skill

Perhaps the most powerful skill we can ever develop is to be *curious* in a challenging situation. This is an inner strength. It is staying open to possibility—not investing in what you think you already know.

"Knowing" is the cement that permanently seals in our misery. It kills love. We know exactly how our partner feels, and what they mean by their words or actions. We couldn't possibly be misinterpreting them. In fact, we don't even realize that's all we are doing—*interpreting* them.

Nothing closes us down faster than being misinterpreted or told what we feel. It's a ticket straight to the Hole.

THE FIVE STAGES OF RELATING

Here's a key parable[1] about how we learn new and better strategies. We learn through trail and error, in stages:

STAGE 1. You're walking down a road and there's a hole. You fall into the hole. You think, "Who put this hole here? Why did they do this to me? I don't deserve this treatment..." You scratch and dig... and finally, with cuts and bruises... you get out of the hole and continue walking...

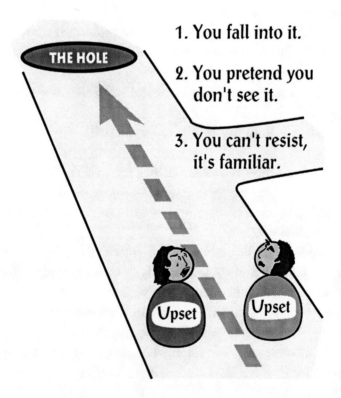

1. You fall into it.

2. You pretend you don't see it.

3. You can't resist, it's familiar.

STAGE 2. You're walking down a road and there's a hole. You pretend that you don't see it. You act as if it isn't really there. So you fall into the hole. You think, "Who put this here? How can they keep doing this to me? This isn't right! They are wrong..." You scratch and dig... and with cuts and bruises... you get out of the hole and continue walking...

STAGE 3. You're walking down a road and there's a hole. You see it. But you just can't resist. It's so familiar... that you jump into the hole. You now think, "How come I always end up here? What is this hole really all about?" You scratch and dig... and finally, with cuts and bruises... you get out of the hole and continue walking...

STAGE 4. You're walking down a road and there's a hole. You see it. You recognize it. You've been in that hole before. You think, "I know this hole! I don't want to go in there..." So you walk around the hole and continue walking...

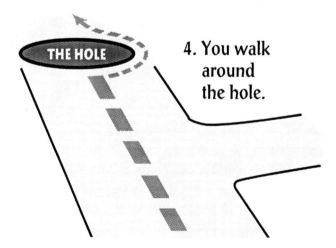

THE HOLE

4. You walk around the hole.

STAGE 5. You're walking down a road and there's a hole. You know that road. You've gone down that road before. You think, "This is the road with the hole in it." So you go down a new road and continue walking...

The parable illustrates the five stages of relating and how we deal with issues, problems or upsets. At first we just find ourselves in a deep hole, and blame someone else for putting us there. Next, we see it but deny it, and fall in again. Third, we see it more clearly, but it seems so familiar and compelling that we jump back in once more.

We start making progress when we see the hole and just walk around it. Finally, we decide to go down a different road altogether. We move toward the unfamiliar, new and unknown. This is the journey of soulmates.

Most of us can easily identify with the story of the Hole. When couples start working with us, we ask them in which "Stage" they currently see themselves. It's usually Stage 3.

We then show couples how to move beyond the grip of the Hole and learn to explore new territory.

The tools offered later in this book will keep you out of the Hole. They are the methods soulmates use to deal with potentially upsetting situations.

We next examine what makes the Hole so familiar and compelling that, even when a couple sees it clearly, they still find themselves jumping in.

WHAT TAKES US INTO THE HOLE?

We follow a "Map" to the Hole. This map is based on the past, on our own personal history.

Think of the map as a metaphor for how the brain learns, organizes and stores our experiences. Our developmental learning process is like the creation of internal maps. Adults use many maps developed in childhood. We have a map for the English language and a map of the letters of the alphabet as visual building blocks of words. These maps enable you to read what you are now reading.

Similarly, we have a map for how to interpret behaviors of others—and how to react. These maps are not always accurate. We easily misinterpret the actions or intentions of others, and not all of our reactions are like soulmates.

Parts of our map take us to the Hole. Especially parts that reference emotional triggers and hot buttons, sensitivities and past wounds, family conditioning, negative beliefs and limiting communication styles.

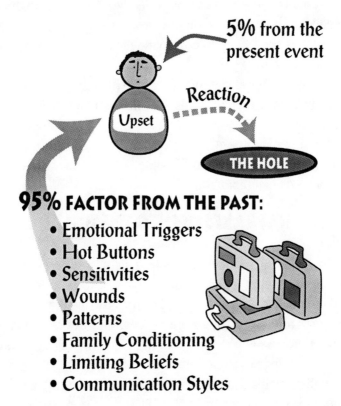

5% from the present event

Reaction

Upset

THE HOLE

95% FACTOR FROM THE PAST:
- **Emotional Triggers**
- **Hot Buttons**
- **Sensitivities**
- **Wounds**
- **Patterns**
- **Family Conditioning**
- **Limiting Beliefs**
- **Communication Styles**

We call these elements the "95% factor" from the past. Another name for it is "baggage." We bring our baggage into new relationships. When something today activates part of our old baggage, we can be taken to the Hole. At such times, we can feel out of control. We suddenly are in the Hole, doing and saying things we would not have done if we were in a calmer, more resourceful state.

There is added emotional intensity in the Hole. This is what the 95% factor refers to. It is like an emotional turbo-charger. It boosts our reaction, accelerating us into a state where we can no longer be constructive.

Another way of looking at the 95% factor is to ask, "Is this emotional response proportional to the event at hand?"

When we are in the Hole, usually only 5% of our emotional energy is proportional to the present event. The rest is about the past. The reactions we are having may not even have anything to do with our present partner.

Recall the example of Sarah and Michael driving to a meeting, where she was being unusually quiet. When he tried to lighten things up by teasing her, she blew up and called him insensitive.

If Sarah's response had been proportional to the event in the car, it may have had only 5% of that emotional energy. At a 5% level, she might have simply said, "Michael, this meeting is on my mind. I need some time to be quiet and prepare for it." Or she might have said, "Please don't tease me. I really don't like being teased."

Instead, the 95% factor from Sarah's past kicked in. Experiencing a big jolt of emotion, she became enraged. Perceiving Michael as the sole cause of her feeling, she made a negative judgment. This, in turn, seemed to him like an unprovoked attack and he became defensive.

They went straight to the Hole.

So what was in Sarah's map from the past? It turned out that the 95% factor was that in childhood, her father often ridiculed Sarah with putdowns in the form of teasing.

Michael unwittingly hit that land mine.

THE MAP FROM OUR PAST HISTORY

The map from the past that takes us to the Hole was created by events where we ended up feeling bad or thinking less of ourselves. These events could have been about something big or little.

The feelings from these events were never healed or resolved, and they continue to influence us today. They are reactivated by anything today that reminds us of the original events in the past.

This is the 95% factor. It is primed and ready to turbocharge any of the emotional responses we have today.

Unfortunately, most of us are unskilled at noticing when the 95% factor kicks in. We don't question the accuracy of our interpretation of the present event. We don't ask how the past is influencing our perception. We may even tend to mistake the strength of our reaction with its accuracy—so the stronger we feel, the more right we are!

If only 5% of Sarah's emotional energy was truly needed for the event in the car, then why couldn't she have just stopped at that and delivered a constructive message to get what she really wanted?

Most likely, she had no idea that she had ever moved beyond the level of appropriate response. Few of us recognize that we are going beyond 5% when it is happening. Perhaps we continue to feel we are responding proportionally, all the way to the Hole.

Soulmates also have maps from the past. They know that they can be reactive. The difference is that they stay alert for going beyond the 5% level. They know that even at 10% you are in danger, because it's a short jump to the Hole.

THE GOOD NEWS

The map is not the territory

The good news is that the *map* is not the *territory.*

How we think things are is not the same as how they really are or what is possible for us to experience.

We do not have to stay limited by our maps. We can learn new things throughout life. To achieve a deep, lasting happiness, you are called on to expand your current map. If you want to go somewhere other than the Hole, you need to discover a new road.

The good news is that you *can* travel on new roads in a

relationship. It can be done! All kinds of new roads are there for you to discover. And the tools in this book will help you find and share them with a loving partner.

Soulmates are open to taking new roads where the old one only leads to the Hole. Consider the following metaphor[8] about the difference between Heaven and Hell.

In Hell, you are taken into a room where there is a giant table full of all manner of wonderful food for a feast. Around the table sit the residents of Hell, frantically scooping up the food. They are using big spoons which are permanently fastened to their hands. But the handles on each spoon are a bit longer than their arms. So they can never reach the ends of the spoon back to their mouths. They are literally starving at a feast, slopping food all over themselves—screaming and moaning with the pain of starvation!

In Heaven, you are taken into a similar room with a giant table set with the food for a feast. Around that table sit the occupants of Heaven. They too have spoons fastened to their hands, each with handles longer than their arms. But here, with their long spoons, these people are feeding each other! Sounds of pleasure and happiness abound.

This is a feast fit for soulmates, who know how to go down a new road and discover mutually satisfying solutions—even in the most challenging of situations.

So the good news is that the map is *not* the territory. We *can* expand and we *can* learn new skills and attitudes that will improve the quality of our love life. Even if we did not get these good lessons in childhood, we can start now.

It takes conscious intention to do this learning. It is vital to know from the start what we are up against.

THE BAD NEWS

- **The map is unconscious**
- **We follow it automatically**
- **It's what is familiar**
- **We mistake the map for reality**

Maps are unconscious and this gives them enormous power. This can be a good thing. Many of the things we learned in the past still serve us well. We learned to look both ways before crossing the street, and to wait for the light to turn green. We now follow that automatically.

But a lot of other things learned in childhood are not necessarily still so beneficial. These are the things which take us to the Hole—the ways we negatively interpret the words and actions of our partner, the ways in which we believe we must react to them.

We can easily mistake our map for reality. Relationships get into trouble when we are upset, and we mistake our interpretations for what is really going on. We place our partner somewhere on our map and mistake that for who they really are. We label them and believe we know just what their intentions and feelings are.

In other words, we turn our partners into co-stars in our old movies. In the example above, Sarah cast Michael to play the role of the abusive father in her old movie. An old script written long ago determined how she reacted to his teasing in the car. Most likely, she didn't consciously realize this. She just reacted, as if he were being abusive.

Sarah made a snap judgment, as we are prone to do.

It can be called the map, our old movies, or our baggage. We are limited by it. It influences how we react to each other and how we end up in the Hole. Soulmates wake up, stay alert, and do not mistake their maps for reality.

Soulmates are wary of making snap judgments, and will even delay judging an event or situation. Perhaps they have learned over time and many painful errors the exact cost of jumping to a reaction. Or maybe they had a sudden insight, like the revelation in the following story[3]:

While on a walk one day, I was surprised to see a man hoeing his garden while sitting in a chair.

"What laziness!" I thought. But suddenly I saw, leaning against his chair, a pair of crutches. The man was at work despite his handicap.

The lesson I learned about snap judgments that day has stayed with me for years now: the crosses people bear are seldom in plain sight.

IN OUR HEARTS, WE WANT FREEDOM!

- **Expand beyond limits of map**
- **Heal old wounds**
- **Realize our dreams of love**

In our hearts, we all want freedom. We want to heal old wounds and expand beyond the limits of the map. We want to realize our dreams and potential for love today.

This is our yearning to be soulmates. We get a brief taste of this expansion during the initial period of a relationship— during the magic and wonder of the honeymoon.

THE HONEYMOON IS LIKE
A VACATION FROM THE MAP

- Temporarily escape the map
- Glimpse a possibility of expansion

The honeymoon is like a vacation from the map. The magical sense of this time is an experience of living beyond our normal maps. It's a visit to a wonderful foreign place. We see a glimpse of expansion—a snapshot of possibility.

Most of us see the honeymoon as "true love"—evidence that we are finally involved in the "real thing" with the "right person." We may feel we have met our soulmate.

But eventually we find out we don't travel that light... We carry old "Baggage"

When we rediscover our old baggage, the honeymoon is over. The arrival of baggage seems like a rude catastrophe, a sign that love has taken a turn for the worse. We may even conclude we are with the "wrong person."

Few couples understand that relationship moves in stages. Old baggage is certain to be rediscovered until it gets healed. In fact, old baggage and wounds may even be emerging into the light of new love in order to be healed.

Here's a little-known secret that wise soulmates know:

Love attracts anything unlike itself.

What's unlike love? Pain—old wounds—deep fears— negative beliefs—all the ingredients of the 95% factor from the past. Love often brings up old baggage for healing and completion.

Expansion and growth can be an integral part of a loving relationship. Wise soulmates see this potential. Hence, they do not deny their old baggage. They know its arrival signals an important time in a shared journey—where old wounds can be healed, old limits can be surpassed, and old emotional patterns can be transformed.

This realization can come suddenly, as it did for Susan. She had been a client for six months, and every week she arrived with a new story of how her boyfriend Paul upset her. She complained about his lack of sensitivity, his inability to express feelings, his unconsciousness in spending time together, and his lack of visual awareness—he was a "slob." She was doing the blame game, saying everything would be great if Paul would just get his act together.

We approached these multiple challenges in a variety of ways, to come to a deeper understanding of what it was that was really upsetting her. She continued to insist that it was all Paul and that she had nothing to do with it. After six months of exploring the same challenges over and over, without the results she was looking for, I gently leaned forward in my chair, and said "Perhaps Paul is not the man for you."

She leapt out of her chair and responded, "How can you say that? He is perfect for me! Nobody pushes my buttons like he does. And if he doesn't push my buttons, how will I ever grow?" She relaxed back into her chair, having an expression conveying that a light just went on in her head.

From that point on, we continued to explore the issues from the perspective of her personal growth, rather than placing the blame on Paul. We now focused on her ability to be aware of what she was feeling, of what she needed and wanted, and how to communicate these in a respectful way. We also focused on exploring where these buttons came from and how to heal them.

Soulmates come to understand a particular wisdom that applies to traveling to any destination—be it geographical or a region of the heart. They understand that the sooner this wisdom is applied, the sooner you can get on with the rest of your journey.

The wisdom is simply this:

 **GO TO BAGGAGE CLAIM AREA**

We discuss this step of the journey next...

CHAPTER THREE

CLAIMING YOUR OLD BAGGAGE

"If you want the present to be different from the past, study the past." —SPINOZA

WELCOME TO THE
BAGGAGE CLAIM AREA

PLEASE PROCEED WITH CARE:

1. LOCATE EACH OF THE PIECES
2. IDENTIFY OWNERSHIP
3. OPEN & EXAMINE CONTENTS

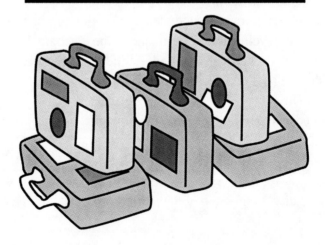

All travellers know about the Baggage Claim Area. We stand around impatiently and wait for our luggage to appear. There is usually a crowd of people competing to be at the front of the line. We are alert to spot our baggage, since it is filled with valuables. We wouldn't want anyone else to mistakenly walk off with our stuff. Nor would we want to leave any of our bags behind.

In relationship, it is usually the exact opposite.

When our interpersonal baggage shows up, we stand around denying it's our stuff. We pretend that everything that gets stacked up in the Baggage Claim Area belongs to our partner—not to us! No, we don't own a single thing there among the stacks and stacks of unclaimed baggage.

THE BAGGAGE CLAIM DILEMMA
Is it yours... or the other persons?

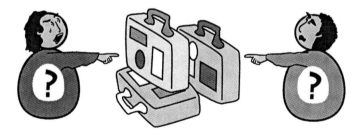

The big dispute in relationship often is: "Whose baggage is this?" Each partner is likely to say, "It's the other person's stuff that's causing the problem here."

The typical statement about baggage is that it's the other person who has something wrong with them, and that is what causes the current problem, upset or challenge.

For instance:

- "Hey, that's your problem."
- "Deal with it!"
- "Get off of it."
- "What's your problem?"
- "You make me mad."
- "You act just like a little child!"
- "I don't know what her problem is."
- "He needs to get his act together!"
- "She never lets up... she's so insecure."
- "He's so insensitive and walled-off."

We focus on baggage that is apparently held by the other person. They need to get their act together, deal with their problems, limiting beliefs or behavioral deficits. They need to change so we can feel better again. All of us tend to have a blind spot for the part we play in a situation, the emotional baggage we carry, and our own 95% factor.

A Tibetan story[4] tells of a meditation student who, while meditating in his room, believed he saw a spider descending in front of him. Each day the menacing creature returned, growing larger and larger each time. So frightened was the student, that he went to his teacher to report his dilemma. He said he planned to place a knife in his lap during meditation, so when the spider appeared he would kill it. The teacher advised him against this plan. Instead, he suggested, bring a piece of chalk to meditation, and when the spider appeared, mark an "X" on its belly. Then report back.

The student returned to his meditation. When the spider

again appeared, he resisted the urge to attack it, and instead did just what the master suggested. When he later reported back to the master, the teacher told him to lift up his shirt and look at his own belly. There was the "X".

THE VIEW FROM CHILDHOOD

- The other person is big and powerful
- Wounds come from the other person
- Needs met or not by the other person

Looking at the other person as the source of upset is built into the baggage itself. Baggage is just another name for the 95% factor, discussed above with the map from the past. This originated in childhood, when "family" created "familiar" behaviors and feelings.

Childhood was a time when the other person, namely our parent, *was* larger than us and more powerful. They were the source of love and nourishment, and the means by which our needs were met—or neglected.

Our childhood experience made the other person the source and cause of our pleasure or pain. When we were emotionally hurt as children, whether our parents intended it or not, they were causally linked to the wound.

Any event today that is even slightly similar to a past wound tends to bring up the energy of that earlier wound. This amplifies our emotional reaction to the current event. Linked to this emotional amplification is the sense of a larger, more powerful person as the source of it.

This process of emotional amplification is unconscious, so

we may not even recognize that it is going on. What we do recognize is that we are getting upset. This becomes the apparent problem for us. What is happening is the 95% factor is kicking in, coming up out of the map of our past.

Most of our emotional triggers, hot buttons, sensitivities, wounds, patterns and limiting beliefs remain linked to the sense of a larger, more powerful other person. We sense that other person makes us feel upset.

Sentences like "You make me angry!" or "You drive me crazy!" seem to be part of the syntax of love. These are one form of the famous "You" Statements. We say them easily—and question them rarely.

By the time we are adults in relationship, we have a fully developed map for what causes our feelings. The cause is almost always seen as being external to ourselves. We do not recognize how our baggage is involved. It clearly looks to us as if the other person makes us feel the way we do.

Soulmates—and philosophers—question what they are *not* seeing. They even question the basic validity of thinking in terms of cause and effect, and how this thinking keeps us from recognizing the larger picture—in which we play an integral part in the events of our lives.

This was well put by the philosopher Alan Watts[5]:

Why is the mutual interdependence between ourselves and the external world not the most obvious and dominant fact of consciousness? Because we look at things separately instead of simultaneously....

We believe that everything and every event must have a cause, that is, some other thing or event.... I can't help what I do. I am simply a puppet pulled by strings.

This... comes from asking the wrong question. Here is someone who has never seen a cat. He is looking through a narrow slit in a fence, and, on the other side, a cat walks by. He sees first the head, then the less distinctly shaped furry trunk, and then the tail.... Thereupon he reasons that the head is the invariable and necessary cause of the tail, which is the head's effect. This absurd and confusing gobbledygook comes from his failure to see that head and tail go together: they are all one cat.

The cat wasn't born as a head which, some time later, caused a tail; it was born all of a piece, a head-tailed cat. Our observer's trouble was that he was watching it through a narrow slit, and couldn't see the whole cat at once.

THEY MAKE US FEEL THE WAY WE DO

We unconsciously transfer the causality of our feelings to our current partners. In the honeymoon, they make us feel great. Then later, they upset us. In many cases, we may even feel small again. We need them to change so we don't have to feel upset anymore.

We often have couples who are involved in strong emotional reactions do an experiment. We ask them to close their eyes and get a quick image or sense of their partner, who is apparently causing their upset feelings. Then we inquire whether they sense their partner is larger, the same size or smaller than they are.

In a majority of cases, they imagine the other person as a much larger person and themselves as small. We then ask them to tell us the last time in their life that was actually the case. Of course, it was when they were children.

Couples are often startled to recognize how deeply ingrained the tendency is to assign an external cause to upsets. We tend to think that it is the other person who is making us feel what we do, and that they are the only ones who can change what we feel.

You know the 95% factor has kicked in and you are headed for the Hole, when the source of your upset appears to be the other person—and you believe that healing or solutions come from outside of yourself.

Soulmates are aware of how easily we place the blame for upset feelings onto others, and act as if the only solution is to get the other person to fix how we feel. The recognition of this process helps soulmates avoid being trapped by it.

WE STILL UNCONSCIOUSLY ACT AS IF HEALING COMES FROM THE OTHER PERSON

- Wanting the other person to change
- Blaming others for how we feel
- Saying they "make" us upset
- Thinking it's 100% about others... not us
- Not recognizing the influence of our past

We want them to change. We blame them for how we feel. We think that whatever feelings are coming up for us here and now are 100% a product of what they are doing.

It's like we put our partner into a movie of childhood, casting them in the role of one of our parents. Then we act out our part in the movie and treat them accordingly.

Recall again the example of Sarah and Michael and his failed attempt to lighten things up by teasing her. She blew up, called him insensitive, and they ended up in the Hole.

Unconsciously, she cast him in the role of her father who teased her abusively as a child. At the moment her 95% factor kicked in she experienced rage in her body. She identified Michael as the sole cause—the only blame for her upset feelings. She verbally reacted to him accordingly.

But Sarah did not recognize that her own past baggage was involved. She did not remember her father. Nor did she sense how wounds from her past amplified her emotions like a turbo-charger, accelerating her ride to the Hole.

Soulmates know that we need to claim our baggage from the past and take an active role in healing it—otherwise it will unconsciously block us from the love we truly want.

Far from disclaiming their old baggage or thinking that their reactions are caused by a partner, soulmates look for their own part in an upset. They know that this will be a route to healing the old wounds and sensitivities which get carried from one relationship to the next.

Like Susan finally realized one day, potential soulmates recognize the power of looking within. As she exclaimed, soulmates will finally see that "if nobody pushes my buttons, then how will I ever grow and heal?" A partner who wants to be in a soulmate relationship will pull up his or her own shirt and look for the "X" on their own belly.

Soulmates are ever alert to look for the active part they can and do play in a relationship. They know the danger and dissatisfaction of assuming a passive viewpoint.

THE PASSIVE VIEW OF RELATIONSHIP

People use a wide variety of metaphors in thinking and talking about relationships. Sometimes relationship is spoken of as if it were a vehicle—a train "off track," a boat "on the rocks," or perhaps a bus "going nowhere."

"This relationship is going... "
• Nowhere
• Straight into the Hole

Most of these metaphors reveal a very passive stance. It's all about the relationship, and where the relationship is going. People talk as if they had no part in it at all. It's almost as if they are sitting in the back of the "Relationship Bus" waiting to see where the bus will go.

Achieving longlasting fulfillment in love requires the active participation of both partners.

WHO IS DRIVING THE BUS ANYWAY?

- Nobody
- The other person
- It's on auto-pilot, set to follow a map based on your past

Soulmates seek to understand their active influence in a relationship. Instead of sitting in the back of the Relationship Bus, they ask, "Who is driving?"

Often, partners may feel that nobody is driving, that the relationship simply has a life of its own. Sometimes, it seems that the other person is driving—"driving us crazy."

In more extreme cases, we may feel like an "innocent bystander" on the road of love, who has just been run over by the Relationship Bus.

Who is driving? Relationships tend to go on auto-pilot, set to follow the map of each partner's past. All baggage is safely tucked out of sight on the roof.

But the relationship is being controlled by that hidden baggage, and the "ghost of the past" is at the wheel.

When upsets arise, it is all too easy to look outside for the cause. People do this unconsciously. Unfortunately, it keeps us from creating deep love and connection.

If you want the fulfillment of soulmates, you will need to come to the front of the Bus, get into the driver's seat, and realize that it's your Bus—and it's a Bus built for two.

Consider the power of a single word. Think about how you are *relating* instead of *the relationship*. "Relating" is a verb, an active process in which you play an active part.

TAKING AN ACTIVE PART IN RELATING

Sometimes, when couples complain about how bad their "relationship" is, we ask them, "How are you *relating* to your partner today?"

Relating is an ongoing active process—not a static object separate from you, like the noun "relationship" implies.

In terms of metaphors, relating is like dancing.

RELATING IS LIKE DANCING

- Each partner plays an active part
- Each partner affects the other
- It is simultaneous
- There are many different dances
- You can actively choose new steps
- There is movement
- Timing is a big factor
- You can learn better balance
- You have two feet

In dancing, each partner plays an active part. The shape and form of the dance can vary over time, and each partner has an affect on the other. Dancing is a matter of movement, timing, balance and footing. All factors come into play.

Partners can explore and learn a variety of new dances.

You are not just stuck with one dance, for instance, the dance to the Hole. Look at the dance the two partners are doing in the illustration. It is called the "polarity polka."

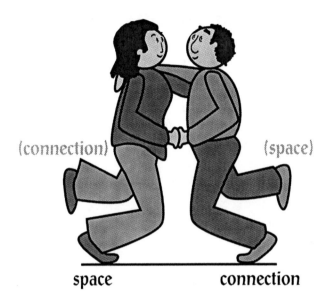

(connection)   (space)

space   connection

The polarity polka is a dance that couples often fall into doing. It is a dance of *opposition*. Each partner puts down the opposite foot of the other. If one puts their right foot down, the other puts down their left.

In this polka dance, the expression "on the other hand" translates into: "on the other foot..."

What we are talking about here is how couples move into opposition as they attempt to deal with difficulties, conflicts, decisions, challenges or upsets. They don't even realize how they do this. It's automatic and unconscious.

The polarity polka is a dance straight to the Hole.

We will discuss at length how to avoid the polarity polka and instead engage in happier, healthier styles of dance. But first we will explore several of the popular polarity polkas that couples commonly fall into dancing together.

VARIOUS POLARITY POLKAS

- **Connection vs. Space**
- **Closeness vs. Distance**
- **"Needy" vs. "Cold"**

One of the most difficult issues in relating is moving between *closeness* and *distance*. If this turns into a polarity polka, a great deal of suffering results and relationships can even self-destruct.

Look again at the cartoon above, of the people doing the polarity polka. In that picture, one foot stands for closeness and connection. The other foot is distance and having your own space. In dancing the polarity polka, if one partner wants distance, the other needs closeness. And if one wants connection, the other needs space.

This elicits a feeling of abandonment in the partner who wants closeness. It brings up a feeling of overwhelm or entrapment in the partner who needs distance. These feelings are turbo-charged by past baggage carried around since childhood. Since most people carry such baggage, this dance is quite common.

Take the example of Jim and Ann.

Jim and Ann came to us in a crisis. Their relationship of ten years was in danger of ending. Jim complained that Ann didn't spend time with him, broke agreements to be together, and that she put more time and energy into her business than she put into the relationship. Ann complained that Jim was needy and insecure. She had to run a business and didn't have time to be with him every time he called.

Over a period of six weeks, we explored their past and how it was influencing them now. What we discovered was that their wounded "inner children" were in charge of their relationship. Their childhood wounds were complementary. Jim had been abandoned as a child and still carried much anxiety and fear. Ann had been overly protected, with her personal privacy often violated by her parents.

After sharing this history and understanding each other, they began to support each others' growth and healing. Each wanted to heal old wounds and learn new behaviors. Jim learned how to give Ann space. And she learned how to be present and stay with Jim, even though her old reaction was to leave in order to get space.

Jim and Ann learned new skills, healed old wounds and rekindled their love. They "popped" their polarity. The issue of closeness and distance lost its charge and they were able to find mutually satisfactory solutions for scheduling their time together and apart.

In the polarity polka, each partner keeps only one foot on the ground. Their other foot is "in the air," or disowned. In reality, everyone needs connection and everyone needs space. A healthy relationship balances both needs. We each have two feet—and need both to be whole.

But in the polarity polka, we pretend to have only one foot, the opposite of our partner's. We look down at our partner's foot as wrong. If they stand on their closeness foot, we may call them "needy" or "insecure." If they stand on their distance foot, we may call them "selfish" or "cold."

By doing this, we create even more pain and push each other to further extremes of opposition. We trigger each other's basic wounds around abandonment or entrapment, in deeper and deeper waves of upset and confusion.

The dance can suddenly reverse, and each partner puts down their opposite foot. Usually the partner pursuing closeness will back off and then the formerly distant partner starts feeling abandoned. They switch roles, trade places—but the pain does not stop.

Soulmates know that there's gotta be a better way to dance! They are willing to work together and explore new options. To improve the quality of their love, they are eager to learn a better sense of balance between their own two feet. Then their movement can be more graceful. They can work with their timing.

In that way, a couple can truly share closeness at times. And at other times, they can enjoy their own space. Both the "me" and the "we" can be nurtured—without friction or threat to the relationship. The dance of soulmates!

• Feeling vs. Thinking
• Emotional vs. Rational
• Emoting vs. Calm

Another common polarity dance is where one partner operates more from *feeling* and the other from *thinking*. So one partner will tend to be emotional in how they respond and decide things, while the other relies on logic and informed reasoning.

When such couples try to make decisions, conflicts can frequently result. Heart and mind can easily be at odds within each of us. This gets played out between two partners in a polarity dance, when one isolates their rational "foot" in opposition to the other's feeling "foot."

In a full-blown polarity dance partners end up finding fault with each other. One person may be called "aloof" or "non-feeling"—while the other may be called "irrational" or "hysterical."

The stereotype of gender differences has it that women are more feeling and men are more rational. In working with many couples, we have found that it can go either way. The real point, though, is that there is always room for expansion. Soulmates do not limit themselves to stereotypes.

- **Emotional Spectrum (anger - hurt - fear)**
- **Specific feelings are OK vs. Not OK**
- **Feelings are Dumped vs. Suppressed**

Many polarity dances are done in the emotional arena. Partners may *specialize* in different feelings, and argue over which feelings are okay versus not okay. One partner may easily display anger, and the other is very uncomfortable feeling it, showing it or even hearing it. The same may be true of the emotion of pain or fear.

We have seen many couples where the following happens. One partner gets hurt but never gets angry. The other partner gets angry but never hurt. Each criticizes the other for having the wrong feelings.

Here it becomes clear that in a polarity dance, people are really fighting over disowned parts of themselves. A whole human has all feelings, but in each of us, some feelings might be consistently suppressed.

According to the gender stereotypes, males and females tend to specialize in different feelings. Boys are trained not to cry and girls not to show anger. When they get together, she may balk at his displaying angry feelings, because she has disowned that emotion in herself. Similarly, he may not be comfortable with her sadness or pain, because he has been cut off from those feelings inside.

When couples do a polarity dance of specialized feelings, one partner ends up feeling the pain for both, while the other carries anger for both. Learning a new dance requires each partner to become more whole, each in touch with their own full human emotional spectrum.

• Nurturing vs. Authority
• Placater vs. Blamer
• Mediator vs. Boss

Another common polarity dance is between *placater* and *blamer*. Placaters want harmony, good feelings, and like to be nurturing. They know what others feel and need. They are mediators. Their body language is hands outstretched, palms exposed, a way of saying, "What do you want or need?"

Blamers tend to look at what people are doing, as far as right or wrong, and tell others how to improve. They are less aware of how others feel. They seem authoritative, bossy or controlling. Their body language is a pointing a finger at the other person, a way of saying, "You are wrong!"

Quite often placaters specialize in hurt feelings, while blamers specialize in angry feelings. We have heard name-calling between partners in this dance include "wimp" versus "bulldozer."

When the couple has children, this dance creates conflict over parenting styles. The nurturer is criticized for being too soft—the authoritarian partner for being too hard.

• Expression and Solution Styles
• Quick vs. Delayed
• Pursuer vs. Cave-Dweller

A polarity dance that creates a great deal of unnecessary suffering in relationship has to do with the way in which couples express their feelings and try to solve interpersonal issues. What is being polarized is their timing—and timing is something that is critical to dance. Here, the couple is trying to dance together, but at different speeds.

Their differences in timing makes it difficult for them to solve issues together. One partner needs time to go within and discover what they ultimately feel. They may not be able to get in touch with this inner information in the presence of strong emotions being expressed by the other person. What helps them get to a solution is time, space and quiet. They can tolerate things not being resolved for awhile.

The other partner quickly knows what they feel. They want an immediate solution. They have a low tolerance for things staying in an unsolved state. They may be more emotionally expressive, and put out "loud" emotions.

In the polarity polka around issue solving, one partner pursues the other for immediate answers. That other partner retreats, or gives in to making premature agreements. When the agreement is premature, there can be resentment and a failure to keep it later.

Polarization over timing will make it difficult for couples to reach agreements, make decisions and resolve conflict. Say one partner needs to express all their feelings before they can access the rational part of their brain.

The partner "on the other foot" tries to prematurely reason things out before a logical solution is possible. This partner may even try to convince the more feeling partner that they shouldn't feel the way they do.

Another dance is where the feeling partner wants to know how the more rational partner feels, right now. The rational partner gets accused of not sharing feelings when in actuality they cannot access what they feel on demand.

The above group of polarity dances are all based on unmatched timing around the speed of accessing feelings. One partner is fast, the other slow. Trying to dance at two different speeds, they step on each other's feet.

Soulmates look for the underlying factor in these kinds of dances, and then make adjustments to come into better balance with one another over the factor of timing.

• High Energy vs. Low Energy
• Driven vs. Laid Back

Another polarity dance occurs with energetic styles. One partner is very high energy and driven, the other more relaxed and laid back. The differences become the target of value judgments and criticism. One calls the other "lazy." They in turn are called "workaholic" or "obsessive."

Soulmates will recognize how a polarity dance is actually

a call for better balance within each individual. But most couples fail to see this and fight it out between one another, as if it were an external battle.

In reality, most of us could probably benefit from a better balance of high and low energy—work and rest—putting out a lot of energy and recharging our batteries.

If we were more willing to see a polarity polka as a call for better internal balance, we could engage in a new form of dance that assisted us each to become more whole.

Perhaps each partner might even be willing to learn from the other those vital new steps that could help them achieve better internal balance and wholeness.

This is exactly the kind of dancing soulmates do.

• Responsible vs. Spontaneous
• "Uptight" vs. "Irresponsible"

Another polarity dance is being responsible versus being spontaneous. This comes up in decision making. Money conflicts often involve this polarity. One partner suffers the label "uptight"—the other "irresponsible."

The need to plan ahead and feel secure may drive one person, while the other wants to live more in the moment. Frequent disputes result when these two very human sides become split between partners in a polarity polka.

Each partner has only one foot on the ground, each provides only one side of the equation of wholeness. Adding the two of them together looks like one whole, healthy and balanced person—who can be both spontaneous and plan ahead responsibly.

The conflict between them is an externalization of each of their internal battles, between a side they are connected with, and a side they are not.

Soulmates recognize that polarity polkas are a result of unclaimed baggage or disowned parts of oneself. They know that a polarity dance between partners is really a sign of the lack of balance within each partner.

- **Perfection vs. Comfort**
- **Orderly vs. Creative**
- **"Rigid" vs. "Sloppy"**

A common polarity polka seems to be between a partner who is more perfectionistic versus one who is more creative or comfort-oriented. This polarization can create conflict over how orderly a home should be kept.

The perfectionist likes order and has a high priority for keeping things cleanly arranged in specific ways. Often they are visually oriented, and like to "keep a tight ship."

Their partner may be a creative cyclone by comparison, with energy for projects but no priority for the visual clean up phase. Another manifestation may be where partner number two is more into feeling comfortable—being feeling based, not visual in orientation—and finds the emphasis on order to be stifling.

Name calling frequent accompanies either form of this polka. One partner is called "rigid" and the other "sloppy." Balance may never be found in an ongoing polarity dance around this issue—as long as each party believes their way of doing things is right, and their partner is wrong.

- **Extrovert vs. Introvert**
- **Social vs. Hermit**
- **Talkative vs. Quiet**

This dance tends to occur when a couple differs in social orientation. Some partners seem to be energized by outward connections, perhaps superficial, with numbers of people. They are very comfortable at parties and public events, and enjoy meeting new people.

Other partners are energized by the one-on-one encounter, perhaps in greater depth and with someone they know well. Meeting new people or being at an event where there are many people is not as comfortable to them.

The more introverted partner may also be very comfortable with silence and spending time alone, while the other partner may find both to be uncomfortable.

Clearly, extroverted and introverted partners can each learn new things from each other. Each can come into a more balanced place within themselves, where they could be more comfortable in the full variety of circumstances. But typically they lock into a polarity dance and begin to criticize each other.

• Visual vs. Auditory vs. Kinesthetic

The final set of dances we will look at are a product of the differing strategies by which people mentally represent information. Some people are very visual, externally as well as internally, and may literally think in pictures. They may be very influenced by the exact look of things. Engineers and graphic artists often have a visual orientation.

Other people are more auditory, and pay attention to the sound of things, the exact words that are said, the tone of voice, and may think more in terms of internal dialogue. They may be very influenced by external sound. Musicians are a prime example of this type of person.

A third type of person may be more kinesthetic, paying attention to their gut impressions and sensing how things feel, and their thinking literally is based on the feeling of things. Dancers and athletes tend to be this type of person.

Most relationships are between partners with different orientations. A visual type and a feeling type may polarize into one or more of the polkas we have discussed above, never recognizing the simple difference that underlies the majority of their conflicts.

For instance, we saw how the polka of perfection versus comfort may result when a visual type is paired with a feeling type. Each of us can develop our senses and expand the ways in which we represent things.

HOW TO WORK WITH DIFFERENCES

Polarity polkas can completely erode your love.

All partners are different, and they have the right to be different. Absolute acceptance of this fact is vital.

Acceptance is non-negotiable for soulmates. That means being accepted—and accepting your partner.

A violet and a rose are very different. Yet each is a perfect creation of nature. The violet doesn't need to make the rose wrong, and vice versa—there is nothing to defend.

Soulmates also know a very powerful secret about differences. They know there's a great potential in having a partner who is different. It gives you the opportunity to expand who you are. It offers you a chance to move beyond your limits—and develop more personal balance and wholeness.

We get a lot of information from the polarity dances we do. Rather than continuing the battle on the outside with a partner, soulmates turn to look within themselves. They take inventory of any wounds, sensitivities and places where they can expand their internal balance.

DECLARING AN END TO WAR

The first step to creating a better dance is to recognize how you are dancing now. You need to clearly see the part you play in it, how each step you now take influences where that dance goes.

Professional dancers use mirrors to clearly see how they are dancing. Relationship is like a mirror. If we look clearly into what is going on, we can see our part in it.

This involves going to the Baggage Claim Area.

Most people have a hard time claiming baggage. They tend to see it in others, but not in themselves. They may have the belief that to find it within is too painful. Or that there's nothing you can do about it anyway.

In relationship, we are more likely to be defensive, rather than being open about having baggage. It seems that if we admitted it, our partner might have something on us, and this may put us at a disadvantage. It seems best to defend or stonewall. This is a great idea for warfare. But how does it help love or nurture our relationship?

At some point, even dedicated soldiers get tired of the battle and yearn for love. They question the need for warfare and want to find a better way to deal with challenges. An example is the story[6] of how to make soup from stones.

Many years ago three soldiers, hungry and weary of battle, came upon a small village. The villagers, suffering a meager harvest and the many years of war, quickly hid what little they had to eat and met the three at the village square, wringing their hands and bemoaning the lack of food.

The soldiers spoke quietly among themselves and then turned to the village elders. "Your tired fields have left you nothing to share, so we'll share what little we have—the secret of how to make soup from stones."

Naturally the villagers were intrigued and soon a fire was put to the town's greatest kettle as the soldiers dropped in three smooth stones. "Now this will be a fine soup," said one soldier, "but a pinch of salt and some parsley would make it wonderful!" Up jumped a villager, crying, "What luck! I've just remembered where some's been left!" And off she ran, returning with an apronful of parsley and a turnip. As the kettle boiled on, the memory of the village improved. Soon barley, carrots, beef and cream had found their way into the great pot, and a cask of wine was rolled into the square as all sat down to feast.

They ate and danced and sang well into the night, refreshed by the feast and their new found friends. In the morning the three soldiers awoke to find the entire village standing before them. At their feet lay a bag full of the village's best breads and cheese. "You have given us the greatest of gifts, the secret of how to make soup from stones," said an elder, "and we shall never forget." A soldier turned to the crowd and said, "There is no secret, but this is certain: it is only by sharing that we may make a feast."

Potential soulmates are those people who realize that the energy wrapped up in criticizing a partner, being defensive or stonewalling is what kills a loving relationship. The results of these strategies, far from keeping pain away, are seen to generate even more pain.

This realization can produce a turning point in some people's lives. They discover that being open and vulnerable is actually empowering. It empowers self-healing, growth, trust, and a deeper sense of connection. And they discover that unexpected rewards flow from claiming baggage—the rewards of greater joy, passion and aliveness.

People on the way to becoming soulmates realize that all unclaimed baggage only continues to affect us from one relationship to the next—until we finally begin to admit it, open it up and share it with each other.

THE ONLY COMMON FACTOR

Erica, a new client, shared during her intake session that she was now in her third significant relationship—she had been married twice and was now with a long term lover. In her first marriage there were many problems and so she eventually divorced him. Her second marriage had similar problems to the ones she experienced in the first marriage and so she ended up divorcing him, as well.

At this point, Erica concluded that the real problem was

men, and decided that it was impossible to have a relationship with a man. Her next relationship was with a woman. To her great surprise, the very same problems came up!

Contemplating this, Erica realized there was only one common factor in all three relationships—and that factor was *her*. Realizing this, she decided to come to counseling to look for and to heal the things within her that were involved in the unhappiness of each relationship. We started by going to the Baggage Claim Area.

We invite and encourage you to explore the claiming of your old baggage. If you are currently involved in a love relationship, doing this with your partner will increase the depth of your mutual understanding. If you are single, you can still claim baggage—with a counselor or a close friend. In doing so, you are better preparing yourself to meet and be with a soulmate in your future.

EACH PARTNER FINDS THEIR OWN PIECES:

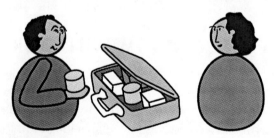

- Opens it up
- Accepts it
- Holds each item up
- Reveals and names it to the other person

Claiming baggage is a shared activity. While one person may be speaking at a time, it is important that both people have their turn. It is an activity that requires a lot of safety. Part of the safety is knowing you are involved in an equal partnership. One of the first things is that both partners must admit that they have baggage.

For many couples, safety is a result of making specific agreements with each other.

Here are typical agreements:

- **Both partners admit they have baggage**
- **Both will explore and reveal their baggage**
- **They will never use what is revealed against each other**
- **Shared info will be kept confidential**
- **When one shares, the other is silent**
- **The atmosphere is non-judgmental**
- **If things get too uncomfortable, you stop**
- **No pushing the other person**
- **Everyone gets all the time they need**

Claiming baggage is an internal activity as well as an external activity. Internally, it is about self-exploration and ownership of what you find. Ultimately, it's about self-acceptance—the acceptance that these are indeed parts of yourself, these patterns and emotional triggers. It's not just the other person's fault. As the Tibetan student did, you are willing to lift up your shirt and see the "X" marked on your own belly.

Externally, claiming your old baggage involves showing the other person what you find. You are willing to name it so that you both understand what is going on inside of you when you are emotionally triggered.

STARTING TO CLAIM BAGGAGE

The act of claiming baggage is as simple as telling stories. The stories relate what it was like to grow up in your family. Give your partner a chance to understand what your past was like and how it influenced you.

Alternate who tells a story and who listens. Tell only what you are comfortable with at this time. Later, you can share more.

Talk about the communication styles that you learned in your family. Discuss the patterns you have recognized in yourself and how far back they go. Look at any sensitivities that may have come out of that early experience.

A good time to share baggage is when you are challenged by someone other than your partner. Describe to your partner what concerns you with that other person. Then let your mind wander, and fill in the following sentence:

"This reminds me of when I was young, and..."

Tell a story about what the current situation resembles in your past. Explore what might be coming up from that past: some old pattern, hot button, sensitivity or wound.

Research shows that a major factor in great relationships is that each partner understands the sensitivities of the other person. Sharing your stories builds this understanding.

WHEN TO CLAIM BAGGAGE

When do you visit the Baggage Claim Area? Consider it a gradual and ongoing process. It is good to set it in motion from the start of a significant relationship. But don't overdo it. Don't start it prematurely, like telling all about your deepest wounds and fears on your very first date.

On the other hand, it's never too late. We have witnessed couples married for thirty years begin to claim baggage, and deep healing and understanding resulted. Years of upsets and issues can be healed in a short time, when partners let down the defenses and claim their baggage together.

Consider the story[6] of the old farmer and the rock. He'd plowed around a large rock in one of his fields for year after year. He had broken several plows on the rock and had grown rather morbid about it over time.

After breaking another plow one day, and remembering all the trouble the rock had caused him through the years, he finally decided to do something about it.

When he put his crowbar under it, he was very surprised to discover that the rock was only about six inches thick and that he could break it up easily with a hammer. As he was carting the pieces away he had to smile, remembering all the trouble that the rock had caused him over the years and how easy it would have been to deal with it sooner.

It is always a good time to start the process of claiming baggage. But be sure and do it when you feel resourceful. If you are very upset, it may not be the best time to try to share baggage, unless you are already very experienced doing so. Of course, when you are very upset, it is not a good time to even try to communicate.

Later, we will talk more about good times to go to the Baggage Claim Area. We will discuss when it's beneficial to talk—and what to do when you are upset. We'll close this section by discussing the benefits we have seen in couples as a result of claiming baggage together.

BENEFITS OF CLAIMING BAGGAGE

- **Leads to healing and wholeness**
- **The 95% factor is reduced**
- **Upset times are shorter**
- **Situations are manageable**
- **Perspective is possible**
- **Mutual agreements can be found**
- **Your relationship is kept clear**

Soulmates know that claiming baggage is an important step towards healing and wholeness.

When you think your upsets are solely caused by others, you are disconnected from the part within yourself that reacts—a part that may be mirrored by the other person. At the Baggage Claim Area, you open things up to name and discover more parts of yourself.

This is an act of ownership and reconnection. To the extent it is done in a safe and loving context, healing can happen. That is why the agreements you make with your partner around claiming baggage are so very important.

As baggage is claimed you can see more clearly when stuff from the past—the 95% factor—kicks into any current situation. By seeing this, it has less power. When stuff from the past has less power, you are freed from acting out conflict with each other. You spend less time being upset, and more time being loving and constructive.

More situations that normally lead to the Hole will be manageable as a result of claiming baggage. You will have greater perspective and will be able to create agreements rather than spinning around the vicious circle, down the spiral, and into the Hole.

PLAYING AN ACTIVE ROLE

Claiming baggage is a major step that says, "Okay, I am a part of what goes on after all." You lift your shirt and reveal the "X" that is marked on your belly. Done in the spirit of improving things, this will empower both you and your partner to actively change what is going on.

Claiming baggage is an act of a soulmate. You are coming forward from the back of the Relationship Bus. You are becoming an active dancer, able to move in new and positive directions.

Always remember to claim baggage in the spirit of mutually improving things. Beware of falling back into the unconscious pattern of assigning blame, of saying, "See, it's your problem after all!" It's not about finding fault.

When you claim baggage, you see your patterns. You recognize emotional triggers. You admit sensitivities. You own hot buttons. You can name how your old wounds are restimulated. You see the role your family conditioning plays. You admit limiting beliefs or communication styles.

At first, this might not seem like a path to empowerment. It is uncomfortable to open up, explore and name such things to your partner. It may even seem like you have to give up necessary power or defensive ability.

But when you let yourself believe it's all their fault, you severely limit your own options. You have no power to heal or change. You are sitting in the back of the bus. The bus is being driven by the ghost of the past. When upsets and challenges occur, the ghost ultimately knows the way to the Hole, and little else.

It will take an act of waking up to really transform a relationship, or your life. Claiming baggage is an important part of this waking up.

BEGIN THE PROCESS NOW

If you are in a relationship, at this stage of reading we recommend that you begin to discuss with your partner the contents of this chapter. If you are single, do this with a willing friend, family member or relative

Create an agreement that supports claiming baggage in the spirit of improving things, rather than finding fault. Discuss what would create safety for each of you—and make agreements to stay safe.

When things are good, people may not see reason to go to the Baggage Claim Area. But if things are calm, you can make clearer agreements and share heartfelt information. It's a great time to discuss what will help you to feel safe and supported in claiming baggage—the perfect time to explore the idea and practice going to the Baggage Claim Area.

CHAPTER FOUR

THE GOLDEN RULE
FOR SOULMATES

*"Insanity is doing the same thing in the same way
and expecting a different outcome."* —CHINESE PROVERB

If a couple thinks of their relationship as a vehicle, they are thinking in a passive manner. Earlier, we talked about one vehicle: a bus. Here we will discuss another vehicular metaphor, relationship as a boat—the "Relation Ship."

- **Sunny skies**
- **Smooth sailing**
- **Everything's ship shape**

When the Relation Ship is "good" you are moving with full sails ahead. The sky is sunny. The waters are smooth. Everything is ship shape. It's a joyful time.

It is also be a good time to go deeper and share matters

from the heart. This can lead to more profound intimacy and fulfillment. Claiming old baggage can be an important part of this exploration. It is a matter of setting sail for deeper waters—and the unknown.

But sometimes, couples settle into a place where they try to avoid all potential conflict or upset. They stay on the surface rather than going deeper. Not wanting to risk upset, they avoid anything that could lead to significant emotions.

Just be sure not to "Rock the Boat!"

Being in an upset-avoidant framework, a relationship can appear to be going okay. Partners can take pride that they never fight. They may put their attention on matters external to the relationship itself, such as childraising, homemaking, career, business, whatever.

But in avoiding their potential to feel "bad," they also limit their potential to feel anything—including "good." Relationships in a state of avoidance often die of boredom.

True harmony cannot come from avoiding things. If you find yourself in such a limbo state, it's a signal that this is the time to learn and expand your relating skills.

The right relating skills can make all the difference. Without these skills, deeper emotions and conflict will lead to destructive behavior. With these skills, however, you will find healing, a deeper connection and stronger passion.

Are your maintaining an apparent state of harmony at all costs? Or can you afford to rock the boat a little, as a part of moving forward?

You don't really achieve anything by not rocking the boat,

other than to let things build up under the surface, not faced and not dealt with. Such things will ultimately come to the surface later, with far more force and power.

Then the Relation Ship can suddenly seem to be "bad." Just as sudden as an unforecasted storm. The waters are choppy and the sky is full of clouds—maybe thunder and lightning. The sun is hidden. You have that sinking feeling.

• Turbulence
• Hole in the boat
• You seem to be
  sinking fast

Often, when couples stay very upset with each other, they begin to describe the relationship as if it's a boat that has a hole in it. They may even feel like they are sinking.

As they describe what is going on, it seems like the most important question to them is figuring out who is causing the challenge they both are experiencing. Of course, each partner blames the situation on the other person.

THE BLAME GAME

A couple could focus on finding a positive solution, one which works to mutually satisfy the wants and needs that are not being met in the challenging situation. But sadly, couples usually tend to place their focus on "What is wrong?" and "Whose fault is this?"

With this usual focus, there is little energy left over for creating a solution or discovering new and possible options. Instead, partners spend all their energy in the misguided attempt to figure out who to blame the problem on.

Essentially, this is like two people in a sinking boat who are only asking one question:

Whose Side of the Boat has the Hole?

Each partner points the finger at the other. Each says it's the other person who is causing the relationship to suffer. Meanwhile this boat they call their love is going under.

Each gets trapped in the blame game instead of grabbing a bucket and starting to bail the water out. Each thinks its their partner's job to do that.

Will finding out whose side of the boat has the hole stop them from sinking? Clearly not. Does this approach work any better for relationships? No!

We have never seen that approach work, in love or at sea. In fact, this approach adds weight to the boat, or the love relationship, and makes it sink faster. Trying to determine whose side of the boat has the hole is the same as going down that same old road and falling into the Hole.

ASK A BETTER QUESTION

Couples can travel a new road when they realize there are better questions to ask. For instance, it will benefit you to question whether the hole is on the outside, external to you. Only when you focus more on what is coming up within yourself, will you begin to go down a new road that can lead to personal healing and wholeness.

Another good question is about the nature of the water that seems to be filling the boat. Water is a symbol for emotions. Again, if you are looking within, you will find that the water is made up of the 95% factor—unhealed wounds, emotional triggers and sensitivities from the past.

Past 95% factor:
It's coming up
and raining down

95%

95%

Perhaps the best question of all is:

What's coming up, asking for healing?

When you ask this question, you can find answers that have the power to transform everything for the better.

The questions you ask will determine the answers you are able to find. This is more than just what you verbalize to each other. It includes the questions that drive how you look at things and think to yourself.

There's an old saying:

"Be very careful what you ask for... because you're likely to get it!"

If you are asking about who is to blame, then all you will get is blame. If you ask, "What's coming up for healing?" then the answers you will get will move you in the direction of healing.

It's like making travel plans. If you only know where you don't want to go, then your travel agent won't know your preferred destination. Similarly, if partners only complain about what they don't like about the relationship or each other, it won't point them to where they *do* want to go.

A negative question only points you toward a negative possibility. "Whose fault is this?" only points to blame. That will never stop the boat from sinking.

Only a positive question points to a positive possibility. Questions like, "How do we get this water out of the boat?" or "How do we fix this hole?"

WE SENSE, DEEP INSIDE OUR HEARTS

- Love can heal
- Love can open us
- We can expand
- The clouds can lift
- The sun is still there

The most important question is: "HOW?"

"How can we heal, open and expand in love?"

Stay with this kind of question. It is very powerful, even if you don't get an answer right away. Keep asking a positive question like this question.

There are many attempts to give recipes for success in love and relationship. There's always some new and inspiring answer. We all want answers. The self-help industry is based on this human desire.

This book, too, presents you with many answers, recipes and recommendations. But for a moment, we would like to pause just a bit longer here and pay homage to the power of asking the right question.

Remember when Susan had the realization that Paul was perfect for her, because "if he doesn't push my buttons, how will I ever grow?" At the moment of that realization, Susan started asking a useful and positive question.

When you keep asking a positive question, it empowers you to find your own best answers. As you ask it, and live it, deep in your heart and soul—you prepare yourself.

LIVING THE QUESTION

Rilke said this well in a poem:

be patient toward all that is unsolved in your heart
and try to love the questions themselves

do not now seek the answers
that cannot be given you
because you would not be able to live them
and the point is to live everything

live the questions now
perhaps you will gradually
without noticing it
live along some distant day
into the answer

Always remember the power of the questions you ask. They drive what you say to your partner. More importantly, questions shape how you think about love and life itself.

In the Chinese language, many written terms consist of two characters that complement or reinforce each other. A relevant term is that for "knowledge." A translation for this term pairs a character meaning "to learn" and one meaning "to question." The former concerns itself with acquiring—the latter with inquiring. Both are indispensable aspects of the process of gaining true knowledge.

In living the question, it is important to have a question worth asking. This is true for the questions we ask when we communicate with our partner. It is equally true for the type of questions we ask ourselves.

Here are some useful and self-empowering questions that you might consider asking yourself, especially at times when there is a challenge or upset in a relationship:

- "Who is driving this bus, anyway?"
- "What is my part in this dance?"
- "What might I not be seeing?"
- "What is coming up from my past?"
- "What do I truly need right now?"
- "What am I assuming about my partner?"
- "What is my partner's positive intention?"
- "What is coming up, asking for healing?"
- "How can we heal, open and expand in love?"
- "Is this going down a new road, or to the Hole?"
- "If I were healed and whole, what would I do?"
- "What would a soulmate do next?"

THE GOLDEN RULE FOR SOULMATES

Here is the simplest and most powerful rule of thumb for relating. It is easy to remember:

If what you are doing does NOT get the love you truly want... then

DO SOMETHING DIFFERENT!

This is one rule you really need to know.

If you keep doing the same old thing, you will keep getting the same old results. You know the road to the Hole and the ways to get there. You also know that every time you apply those same ways, you end up in that same Hole. That's the road that leads to the Hole.

Doing something different is taking a new road. Instead of playing out your normal reaction to an event or situation, do something different. This is the only way you will ever end up in a different place.

It takes courage to do something different, because you won't necessarily know what the right thing is. There may be no one right thing. You can only do this, do that, and see how it works. You cannot know in advance if a particular thing will work.

You are traveling down an unfamiliar road. Know that it will likely be uncomfortable, at least for awhile. It will require you to expand your resources and skills. It will challenge you to face your fears and stretch your limits.

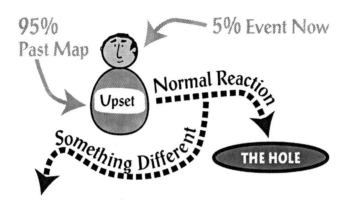

EXPAND YOUR MAP!
- Take a new and different road
- Access your courage
- Move beyond the fear
- Go towards the unfamiliar
- Do this even if there's discomfort

When is the best time to do something different? The signal to do something different is when what you normally do will likely take you to the Hole.

You already know those times. So name them and then stay awake. Figure out what you will do differently when you are in similar situations in the future.

Then do it.

Doing something different is creative and proactive. It is the key that opens the door to the quality of love you want—a passageway out of the Hole and into your dream.

THE SEVEN HABITS OF SOULMATES

1. NAME WHAT YOU WANT TO CHANGE. Name the interactions with your partner that take you to the Hole. Review each one—and answer these questions: What does your partner do? What do you do? What do you feel? What do you need? What do they feel? What do they need? Don't guess—ask them what they feel and need.

2. CLAIM YOUR BAGGAGE. Discuss these interactions with your partner. Do this when you're outside the Hole and share the intention of claiming baggage to improve things. If you cannot stay out of the Hole with your partner, discuss the problem situations with a friend or counselor. The other person is there to listen. You do most of the talking—and specifically cover the six questions above.

3. SEE YOUR ROLE. Get a clear sense of your part in the problem. What specifically do you do in the interaction that adds fuel to the fire? Ask your partner for ideas, or the other person you are discussing things with. Review the section on polarity polkas and identify any dance that's a part of your problem interaction. Name your role in that dance.

4. NAME THE DIFFERENT BEHAVIOR. Name what you'll do in the future that will be different. Start by asking, "What is the exact *opposite* of what I normally do?" See the following examples for ideas. If you are truly brave and can receive feedback not as demands or criticism, ask your partner for ideas of what might work better.

5. **PRACTICE.** Don't wait for things to fall apart before you do something different. Under pressure you can forget everything! Be proactive. Set the wheels turning. Find a small circumstance each day that allows you to practice your new behavior. This will help solidify your learning it.

6. **STAY AWAKE.** Be alert. Don't fall asleep at the wheel. When you find yourself in this type of situation again, see it ahead of time! If you're heading to the Hole, wake up!

7. **TAKE THE LEAP.** You may get upset just like always. It may be very hard to do anything different. The Hole may be calling you on a molecular level. That's okay. Go ahead and do something different anyway. It's the only way out!

Here are some examples of doing something different:

 **SOMETHING DIFFERENT!**

THE HOLE	SOMETHING DIFFERENT!
Urge to get closer.	Allow some space
Urge to escape	Stay there
Urge to resolve now	Allow some time
Express all feelings	Contain feelings
Hold in feelings	Express feelings
Silent about needs	Voice your needs
Get defensive	Just listen
Try to fix or correct	Just listen
Polarize with partner	Hear their truth

ALLOW SPACE. If you sense your partner is distant and your part of the polarity polka is based on a need to get closer, then something different for you would be to allow space—pull back and be with yourself for awhile.

This is especially important around the feelings of abandonment, a red flag that you are in your 95% factor. When you feel your partner is not paying you enough attention, you may normally try to close the gap and pursue a connection. This seems to be the way to stop upset feelings of abandonment, but it takes you to the Hole.

Something different is to step back, breathe, center yourself and allow space to be there. Developing this one simple skill will change the relationship. It is your own inner key to transformation!

Remember the way that Jim and Ann transformed their relationship and themselves. They first went to the Baggage Claim Area and told the stories of where their sensitivities for space or distance originated. After naming their patterns, each of them started to learn to do something different.

Jim faced his abandonment issue. Instead of going to the Hole when Ann needed space for her business, he learned to allow that space—and then take care of his own needs. This resulted in deep healing for him. Meanwhile, Ann responded by wanting to find more time to spend together.

STAY THERE. If your part of the dance is based on the need to escape a situation, then something different is to stay there. This is especially true around the feeling of being trapped or wanting to avoid being around emotions, a sign of your 95% factor.

When the situation could potentially bring up certain feelings, you may normally get nervous or just have to leave. You may space out, try to escape in other activities, or even leave the room. You might stonewall or act avoidant in some other way. You may be driven by fear.

Something different is to breathe, center yourself, and simply stay present. There's nothing else you "have to do" while staying there. Just remain present. Developing this one simple ability will change the relationship. It is your personal key to growth.

Ann's part of the pattern with Jim was to want her space for work, but then to need even more space as Jim would get upset about their lack of time together. Her issue was the need to escape a sense of entrapment or control. As she faced her discomfort, she learned to just stay when Jim wanted to share his feelings. In doing so she learned something that was very healing inside herself. Meanwhile, Jim responded with increased ease when she needed space for her business.

ALLOW TIME. If you normally need to resolve a disagreement, upset or conflict immediately, and your partner shows signs of fatigue or needing space, then allow time before a solution is found.

A sure ticket to the Hole is when one person is demanding an answer or resolution before the other is ready. A partner may need time and even space to get in touch with their own truth. To keep going on, pursuing them, will only lead to the Hole.

Something different is to allow them time. Just sit with the situation not being resolved. Step back, breathe and center yourself. Developing this skill will change things.

Remember the story of the boy and the turtle. Pursuing the turtle with a stick was not the way to get it to open. It only went deeper into its shell. But when the boy could just let the turtle have the time to gradually warm up, it popped its head out and started moving.

Allowing time is to face your own sense of urgency for an external resolution. In sitting with the discomfort, and learning to take care of yourself in the meantime, you will discover a powerful healing within. You will also discover that by allowing time, you can reach better solutions.

CONTAIN FEELINGS. If you normally trigger your partner when you express feelings, then practice the art of containing your emotions instead of blurting them out.

Take anger. If you tend to blow up, then contain your anger. This is the old "count to ten" and then some. Leave the situation. Say you need to take a "time out." Then go somewhere else and do something else. Physical activity is good. Don't bring up the subject until you can discuss it with more clarity and calm.

Containment also applies to other emotions, for instance feeling hurt, abandoned or controlled. If you normally go on and on, acting out these feelings with your partner, it's a sign of the 95% factor. To your partner, it may feel like you are pushing them into a corner. That leads to the Hole.

Something different is to contain your feelings. Go somewhere else and sit with your feelings. Allow yourself to feel whatever you feel, instead of having to "get it out" by expressing it. As you sit with your feelings, focus on how you can best nurture yourself. Embracing your feelings like this can lead to healing and wholeness within. Developing the skill of containment is a key to changing everything and going down a new road.

Containment is demonstrated in the story[4] of a legendary monk. The students in his monastery were in total awe of this elder monk, not because he was strict, but because nothing ever seemed to upset or ruffle him.

One day they decided to put him to a test. A bunch of them very quietly hid in a dark corner of one of the hallways, and waited for the monk to walk by. Within moments, the old man appeared, carrying a cup of hot tea.

Just as he passed by, the students all rushed out at him screaming as loud as they could. But the monk showed no reaction whatsoever. He peacefully made his way to a small table at the end of the hall, gently placed the cup down, and leaned against the wall.

Then he cried out with shock—"Ohhhhh!"

EXPRESS FEELINGS AND NEEDS. If you normally have a hard time expressing what you feel, something different for you is to verbalize, to share your feelings out loud.

Similarly, if you normally do not express your wants or needs, then something different for you is to verbalize, to ask for what you want or need.

Your partner may sometimes ask you what you feel, and you may tend to avoid trying to talk about it. You might be uncomfortable with emotions in general. Or you may know what you need or feel, but hold it all in. Perhaps you do not want to rock the boat—avoiding potential upsets or conflicts.

Something different for you is to articulate your feelings. Ask for what you want or need. You may stutter and stumble and sound foolish. That's okay. You may risk your partner reacting. That's okay. Developing the skill to verbalize your feelings, wants and needs is your inner key to getting the love you truly want.

Laurie was freshly out of a painful two year relationship. She came to counseling knowing that some of her behaviors had contributed to the pain she experienced. In discussing her past she revealed she was one of eight children and learned very early that her parents were not available for emotion support.

If she was in emotional pain, she withdrew and isolated herself. She learned how to nurture herself, but did not learn how to share her pain with another and receive support. We discussed "do something different" — and her something different was to ask for support when she was in emotional pain, and then be open to receiving it.

She had just begun to date Randy. One evening she was upset and afraid. She decided to take a risk and ask Randy if he could come over and offer support. She made the call and to her surprise, there was silence on the other end. Randy calmly explained that he could not come over, that he had a pattern of rescuing women in distress and he was trying to break that pattern.

Laurie thanked him and hung up the phone. She smiled to herself as she realized that it didn't matter whether Randy came over or not. Her growth and healing was in *asking* for support. She also saw how patterns complement each other and offer an opportunity for both partners to heal.

JUST LISTEN. If you normally try to defend yourself in an interaction, then stop and just listen. Or if you try to fix your partner, trying to make them feel better, then stop and just listen to them.

Often, a trip to the Hole is quickened by one partner trying to change the other. This could be done in the attempt to defend yourself from what they are saying about you. Or it could be inspired by the intention to make them feel better.

Either way, you are interrupting them and attempting to enforce your point of view over theirs. This leads to some kind of right versus wrong scenario, where your partner has to lose or end up feeling unvalidated or unheard.

Your partner may then give up trying to communicate—feeling disconnected. This does little to enhance your mutual love life, and can do long term damage. Or if they have the tenacity, they may keep repeating their message until they think you hear them—which will not happen until you stop trying to convince them they're incorrect.

Something different for you is to just listen. Be quiet and hear whatever they have to say. You don't need to defend or explain yourself. You don't need to take care of their feelings or try to change what they are thinking in any way. Just breathe, center yourself, and listen. Maintain eye contact as much as possible. This skill will be your key to changing everything and finding a new road to travel.

Most people are amazed to discover that doing *less*—just being silent and listening—actually does so much *more* to improve the quality of their love.

The wisdom of listening is not a new idea. In ancient Greece, the philosopher Xenocrates stated, "I have often regretted my speech—but never my silence."

Here's a story[6] to reinforce this point:

A police officer in a small town stopped a motorist who was speeding down Main Street. "But officer," the man began, "I can explain..." "Just be quiet," snapped the officer. "I'm going to let you cool your heels in jail until the chief gets back." "But, officer, I just wanted to say...," "And I said to keep quiet! You're going to jail!"

A few hours later the officer looked in on his prisoner and said, "Lucky for you that the chief's at his daughter's wedding. He'll be in a good mood when he gets back." "Don't count on it," answered the fellow in the cell. "I'm the groom."

HEAR THEIR TRUTH. If you normally polarize with your partner, then something different is to hear their truth. This is a deepening of the skill of just listening. It is where you can actually repeat back to your partner, in their words, what you heard them express.

It's not about translating their message into your words. It's not about outdoing them by saying, "I know exactly what you mean. You think that's something, listen to what happened to me!"

This skill is being able to openly inquire, "Tell me more about that." And saying, "That is really something." This skill will be a key to the transformation of your relationship. It can reveal to you a new road to travel together. There is nothing as validating as to truly be heard. Soulmates know the depth of this human need—and how to meet it.

DEVELOP A LOVE COMPASS

N = New road

S = Same old...
S = Stop!

S = Something different is needed... now!

When you are traveling in unfamiliar territory, it helps to have a compass. So if you want to become soulmates and travel down a new road, you need a "Love Compass."

How do you know when to pull out your compass? For some, the signal is that they are starting to feel upset. With others, it's a sense that something is slightly off in how things are going. For still others, it's the recognition that a familiar pattern is starting up that leads to the Hole.

There are two marks on the compass: "N" and "S."

They don't refer to North and South.

N stands for "New road"—where you want to be.

S stands for "Same old..." so "Stop!" and do "Something different... now!"

What is the Love Compass, really? It is *being conscious.*

CHECK YOUR COMPASS EVERY 10 SECONDS

Beware — be aware — get very conscious
whenever you sense you are heading
anywhere near the Hole.

If you even think you are anywhere near the Hole, it's time to pull out your Love Compass. Check it every 10 seconds, because that's how quickly couples can fall into the Hole.

As you check your compass, sense whether what you are about to say or do will take you **N** or **S**—to a New road or to just the Same old...

Check your compass before you say or do another thing. Use it for navigating to a New road.

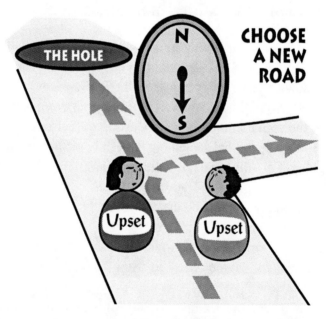

If your Love Compass is pointing to **S**, you need to Stop and do Something different. Try anything different. Do the opposite of what you would normally do. If you are uncomfortable with that, it probably means you are headed in a better direction. It is uncomfortable to do something new and unfamiliar.

DO ANYTHING DIFFERENT

- Say "Stop!" and take a Time Out.
- Do the opposite of what you normally do.
- Ask, "What would I do if I were totally resourceful, healed and whole?"

If nothing seems to work, just say "Stop!" and take a Time Out. We discuss this in greater detail later in this book.

A good thing to do is the *opposite* of what you would usually do. What you usually do takes you to the Hole. Try the opposite thing—and see what happens. We gave you examples in the areas of closeness vs. distance, expressing vs. containing feelings, just listening vs. defending, blaming or fixing, and hearing your partner's truth.

But these are not the only areas of relating where you can benefit by doing something different. Pick any situation that puts you in the Hole. Next, see your part in it. What do you say or do that contributes to the upset? That's where you want to do something different. So what is the opposite of what you usually say or do?

Another way to explore doing something different is to ask yourself, "What would I do if I were totally resourceful, healed and whole?" Imagine how someone else who was centered and confident would behave. Then do that—even though you may not feel centered yourself.

You will be uncomfortable going down a new road. It is unfamiliar. It is different. Feeling uncomfortable is a sign you are going in a new direction.

Remember the story of Sarah and Michael, the couple who

were driving in the car, where he teased her and she blew up at him.

Michael's part in the trip to the Hole was to get defensive and think "I'm only trying to lighten things up. Her behavior is totally inappropriate and wrong." Then he blew up back at Sarah. Down the Hole the went.

Something different for him would have been to identify the feeling, "Wow, I see you are angry." Then ask, "What is going on for you right now? Did I say or do anything?"

Next, instead of trying to defend himself, or trying to fix how she felt, or blaming her for being upset—he could have just listened. He could have held his tongue for five minutes, let her speak, and done absolutely nothing else.

Sarah's part in the trip to the Hole was to have a knee-jerk reaction when a 95% factor kicked in from her past. The energy of an old wound suddenly came up, but not realizing this, she thought Michael was the sole source of her upset.

Something different for her would have been to contain her feelings. Her usual reaction to anger was to immediately and fully express it. If she contained her emotions, she would have been able to process them herself for awhile and then recognize their true source within her.

She might have said, "Your teasing brings up very painful emotions from my past. My father used to abusively tease me as a girl. Anger and hurt from that time is coming back up for me now..." In telling the whole story, going to the Baggage Claim Area, she might have initiated a trip on the road to Healing rather than the road to the Hole.

Such new behaviors would have brought them closer together and put them solidly on the path of soulmates.

DIFFERENCES THAT MAKE A DIFFERENCE

To transform your relationship and act like soulmates, you have to do something different in situations that normally trigger you and damage your love. There are two differences that will give you the most power in the face of challenges.

1. YOUR SHARED VISION

The intention you hold—and how you view what's going on...

When faced with Challenges and Upset.

The first place you need to be different is how you see and think about things—your perspective, your attitude, and the intentions you bring to life in challenging situations.

We strongly recommend that couples consciously align themselves in this key area. It adds invaluable strength to your relationship. We call this having a *shared vision.*

How you view a challenging situation and the intentions you set shape the course of your relationship. This alone will determine whether you constructively resolve challenges and upsets—or get stuck in their negativity.

Couples are seldom conscious of how this operates. But it is a powerful predictor of success in a relationship. So in the next chapter we will cover shared vision in depth.

You will discover the power of your personal vision—and learn how to create a shared vision with your partner. You'll find about shared visions that make a positive difference, and the agreements you can make to support them.

2. THE ROAD YOU TAKE

How you
act, talk,
and express
your feelings...

THE HOLE

When faced
with Challenges
and Upset.

The other key difference you need to make is the road you take. This is how you act, talk and express your feelings, especially when faced with challenges or upset. Up until now, we have talked about this as not going to the Hole, doing something different and taking a new road.

After the chapter on shared vision, we present specific behavioral and communication techniques that will support you to travel on your new road.

Both of these areas of relationship are important. Like in the famous song, they "go together like a horse and carriage." Shared vision is consciously naming the road you want to be on, and voicing that as a clear intention. The road you take is then walking the talk—making the step by step changes in what you say and do, so that you are truly traveling on the new path you choose.

CHAPTER FIVE

THE POWER OF A SHARED VISION

*"If you don't know where you are going,
any road will get you there."*—LEWIS CARROLL

How you view events affects how you respond.

Say you are waiting in a line at a movie. Suddenly, some guy in a heavy coat crashes his way through the line, steps on your foot, never looks back, but just keeps marching along. How do you think you'd react to this?

Next, the person in front of you points out that the guy has a white cane and is bumping into other people. His head turns to the side, and you indeed see he has dark glasses on. What would your reaction be to this new information?

Finally, the person in line behind you says, "That guy comes crashing through here every night. He carries that cane, just pretending to be blind, so he can get away with it." Okay, now what do you think your reaction would be?

With each new view of what is happening, your response may significantly change. The same thing is true in love and relationship. How you view what is going on determines the way in which you will respond.

When a challenge or upset occurs, how you view it may point you down the road toward the Hole. But a different view of what is happening may point you to new road that can take you onto deeper joy and fulfillment.

The power of a viewpoint is increased when both partners see it and share it—when it's a "shared vision."

In exploring the area of shared vision, we are specifically interested in how a couple views a challenge or upset. This is where your vision is of major importance.

Is it a Problem... or an Opportunity?

How you view Challenges & Upset determines the road you'll take.

To simplify matters, how you view a challenge or upset comes down to one central question:

Do you see it as a problem—or an opportunity?

Is the glass half empty or half full? If your focus is on the emptiness, you may needlessly die of thirst. If you focus on its fullness, you can drink, nurture and refresh yourself.

The Chinese language contains many written symbols that have complementary meanings. The most well-known of such Chinese characters is "Wei ji"—the symbol for crisis. It actually consists of two parts: one that represents danger—the other means opportunity.

Whether you see a challenge in terms of being a problem or an opportunity will dramatically impact your response. If you see it in negative terms, the energy you bring into the relationship will also be negative.

Since challenges and upsets are inevitable, your shared vision will make a big difference as to whether love prospers and flourishes—or dies.

"Nothing is good or bad, but thinking makes it so," the old master said[7]. When asked to explain he said, "A man cheerfully observed a religious fast seven days a week. His neighbor starved to death on the same diet."

SHARED VISION AND GOALS

Before jumping into any details, let's look at how we are using the term "shared vision." Many times, couples assume the term shared vision is about the various goals they share, such as "spending quality time together"—"being happy"—"building a great lifestyle."

Shared vision, as we use the term here, is different than such goals. It specifically refers to how you view, understand, and think about the meaning of challenges and upsets in your love life. And the resulting intentions you bring to life.

How you view challenges and upsets will be the primary influence in whether you will share the road to the Hole, or travel a new, fruitful road together as a couple. The attitude and understanding you bring to challenges and upsets will affect your entire relationship—regardless of whatever other kinds of goals you might share.

In this sense, shared vision will even affect how well you ultimately meet your goals. Most goals will involve challenges and upsets. Your shared vision can be a source of tremendous strength in facing any challenges—or not, depending on the nature of how you view them.

For instance, if "being happy together" is your goal, and for some reason you're upset—then you will likely conclude that you are failing at your goal and become more upset.

Good business leaders, in the pursuit of very practical goals, know it's important for people to share a higher vision of what they are doing together. They know that such a shared vision can empower success, and it will help a group face and overcome big challenges. It is similar in relationship.

We will examine the types of shared visions that empower couples to travel a new road, and deepen their fulfillment in being together. But first, we will look at the vision that most of us unconsciously share. It points us to the Hole. We call this the "familiar" shared vision.

FAMILIAR UNSTATED SHARED VISION

Most of us look at challenges, upsets or differences as a "bad" sign. These are seen as unwanted interruptions to love and happiness.

This familiar shared vision is how a majority of people see challenges. It's presented by family and friends, songs and movies. This is a shared vision we never consciously discuss or choose. We are not even aware that we could have a choice! It is like water to a fish, or air to a bird. It is just the way things are—how could they be any different?

The familiar shared vision is that upsets mean something is *wrong*. It could be something "wrong" with your partner, who is seen as the cause of the upset feelings. It could be that something is "wrong" with the relationship. Or, if you tend to think you are responsible, you may even conclude there's something "wrong" with yourself.

It means that **"SOMETHING IS WRONG"** with the Relationship... or You... or Me...

This is undesirable... need to fix it... get rid of it... or get distance...

Wherever it is located—in your partner, the relationship or yourself—something is definitely "wrong." Whatever it is, it is undesirable. Your intention becomes to fix it, change it, get rid of it, or get distance from it—and the relationship.

If we conclude the "something wrong" is located in our partner, then we usually end up blaming or criticizing. If we think it might be located in ourselves, we may get defensive. If we believe "something is wrong" with the relationship, we may close off and distance ourselves.

Reacting to the vision that "something is wrong" does the actual damage to love. Blaming, criticizing, defending and shutting down are the destroyers of a relationship.

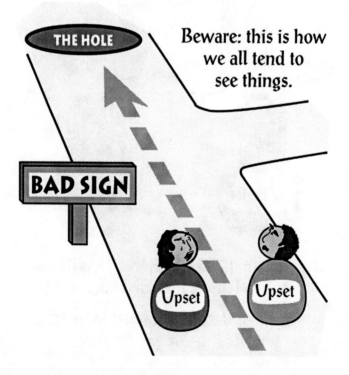

As soon as challenges or upsets are seen as a "bad" sign everything else follows. You will think something is "wrong" and need to figure out who to "blame."

Seeing an upset or challenge as a "bad" sign only leads to the Hole. The sign says, "Go directly to the Hole! Do not pass Go! Do not collect $200!" In effect it says, "Do not find a positive alternative that will strengthen your love!"

Beware! This way of viewing upsets is a product of our past training. We learned it when we learned to walk and talk. It is familiar in origin, passed on from our family of origin.

We saw that upsets, differences and challenges led to reactions. We learned how to react in various circumstances— to find the blame, to criticize the other person, to blow up, to defend ourselves, or to shut down when upset occurs.

Different partners may specialize in various tactics and skills, but we all share the same familiar vision, that upsets are "bad." This is a road sign that points straight to the Hole.

NEW & CONSCIOUS SHARED VISION

If you want to travel a new road, you need to share a new vision. This requires you to consciously explore, discuss, and choose a new viewpoint. You need a different way to view relationship challenges—one that supports you to respond to them constructively and get positive results.

When we first approach this topic with couples, they may come up with shared visions like, "Let's just be happy" or "Let's spend more quality time together." These may be great goals, but they do not guide you to view an upset or challenge in a new and useful way.

To be effective, a new shared vision needs to serve as the basis for understanding—in a new, constructive way—what is going on when upsets or challenges arise.

Here is an example of a useful viewpoint:

It means that "AN OPPORTUNITY FOR PERSONAL GROWTH IS AT HAND"

This is okay... a positive sign... you can work with it...

If there is an upset or challenge, it means that this is an opportunity for *personal growth*. What kind of growth? Keep an open mind. There are many kinds of growth.

For instance, a past wound may have been triggered and is now coming up for healing. Or maybe an old pattern is running and you can now finally learn to expand beyond it.

These are all positive things. They give you a new road to travel—a road that leads to "Growth."

Viewing upsets or challenges as opportunities for personal growth opens that new road up for you. Sharing this vision helps you to set your intentions in a constructive direction.

By seeing any upset that comes along as an occasion for growth, your love and your map will expand.

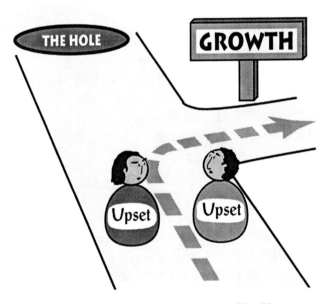

This way of viewing Upset & Challenges leads you to... Expand your MAP!

Sharing a useful vision is the single most important factor in relating. It has a power that goes beyond any skills you can learn for better communication or conflict resolution.

Shared vision provides the basic framework by which you

comprehend what happens. It is the virtual lens through which you see and understand the meaning of events. It directs the manner in which you will respond—or react—to each event.

Like the perception of the guy who crashed through the line at the movies, shared vision supplies the meaning of what just happened. One vision was that the guy was blind, doing the best he could. The other was that he was trying to upset people in line. You will react according to the perception you have of the event, as in this story[8]:

The only survivor of a shipwreck was washed up on a small, uninhabited island. Every day he anxiously scanned the horizon for help, but none was forthcoming. Exhausted, he eventually managed to build a little hut out of driftwood to protect himself from the elements, and to store the few valuables he had been able to take from the wreck.

But then one day, after scavenging for food, he arrived home to find his little hut in flames, the smoke rolling up to the sky. The worst had happened—everything was lost! He was stunned with grief and anger, ready to end it all.

Early the next day, however, he was awakened by the sound of a ship that was approaching the island. It had come to rescue him. "How did you know I was here?" asked the weary man of his rescuers. "We saw your smoke signal," they replied. Remember, the next time your hut seems to be on fire—it just may be a smoke signal that will save you.

In a relationship, your shared vision affects how you react to events. Usually, when the event is that you are getting upset—all bets are off! The familiar shared vision we bring to relationship is that upset is a sign that something is wrong. So we react by going to the Hole.

This is why the term shared vision is not the same as goals like "creating a great lifestyle" or "spending quality time together." Most couples have such goals, but when they get upset, these goals offer no guidance. Under the stress of upset, such goals may even seem irrelevant.

For a shared vision to empower couples, it must provide an understanding that will inspire them to face challenges in a new and positive way. "Healing" is one such vision. It says that being upset is actually an opportunity for healing.

A PACT BETWEEN SOULMATES

Shared vision will be powerful to the extent that it taps into your highest aspirations and spiritual perspective. A shared vision is a pact, made between soulmates. It provides the answer to the question, "What are we here to do in life together, really?"

The familiar shared vision gives a superficial answer— "We're here to have fun and be happy, or blame each other if we aren't." Being upset or challenged is not a part of the vision. It is seen as an obstacle to the goal. Therefore, when upsets and challenges come along, the couple has no guiding light to point towards any positive result.

There's an old Japanese saying:

"The obstacle is the path."

This is an example of viewing challenges in a way that can lead to positive results. Every relationship includes challenges. Our unconscious, familiar vision does not point us anywhere useful, just to the Hole. It does not take us to the paradise we briefly glimpsed in the honeymoon.

Normally, couples in the honeymoon think "This is it!" Anything that follows, where upsets happen, is undesirable. The familiar state of relationship, after the honeymoon, is to lament the loss of the magic—and to resent the apparently unresolvable persistence of upsets and challenges.

We normally view upsets and challenges in that negative light. This disconnects us from our higher intentions. It also disables us from responding in a positive direction.

But upsets and challenges are inevitable.

If we truly want to go down a new and positive road, we need to share a new vision. We need to find a new way of viewing upsets and challenges—a vision that points us to the positive opportunity in each upset or challenge—a vision that brings our highest intentions to life.

It is said that if couples share a deep enough love, they will be able to face anything. Well, love is not enough. If you want to share lasting happiness, plan for the challenges. Make a plan that will guide you in turning each challenge into an occasion that strengthens your love.

In this sense, know that your hut will occasionally be put to the test of fire. Soulmates share a large enough vision to see that such tests are inevitable—and valuable opportunities to grow, heal and become more whole.

The visions that soulmates share provide strength in the face of challenges—when most couples would go the Hole. Shared vision helps couples find their way through the darkness. It gives a new meaning to the currently popular phrase, "What you *see* is what you *get.*"

A VARIETY OF VISIONS

Here are some shared visions that empower and uplift partners in relationship:

- **Personal Growth**
- **Wholeness**
- **Freedom**
- **Healing**
- **Presence**
- **Balance**
- **Inner Peace**
- **Being Clear**
- **Self Realization**

The shared visions on the list above point to higher aspirations. They reach out toward spiritual ideals.

Each of these visions are significant on a personal level. Growth is something we want in our lives as individuals. So is wholeness, freedom, healing, inner peace, self-realization, balance—and all the other things on the list.

A shared vision is a combination of compelling individual visions. It is not something cooked up for the relationship. To be effective, a shared vision needs to tap into what is personally meaningful for you.

Partners do not necessarily have to use the same word for a shared vision. All the words on the list above point in a similar direction. Partners can share a vision that combines what is personally compelling to each of them.

Many couples have committed to a shared vision that includes more than one word, like "Healing and Wholeness" or "Personal Growth and Balance." Articulating a shared vision is an open and creative process.

Here are some qualities of a shared vision that will give it the most power:

A GOOD SHARED VISION

- Embraces all challenges that take you to the Hole.
- Helps you see these challenges in a new, positive light.
- Moves you to be joined in a common, meaningful goal.
- Supports courage to face challenges.
- Helps you to be constructive rather than going into the Hole.

Check out the strength of your shared vision by how well it does with the five criteria listed above. A good vision can embrace all upsets and challenges. It's an umbrella that reaches over all things that normally lead to the Hole.

At first, some couples have a restricted vision. They may think, "Healing is great when it comes to upsets like feeling abandoned. We see how that goes back to childhood wounds that need to be healed. But when it comes to money issues, well that's something entirely different!"

It's important that your vision embraces everything that

normally takes you to the Hole. It covers issues over money, sex, power, childraising, picking a new car, whatever...

A good shared vision will embrace any challenge and let you see it in a new, positive light. It will move you to be joined in a common, meaningful goal. It will support your courage to face the challenge and be constructive with one another instead of going to the Hole.

Does a shared vision solve all problems? No. There are "deal breakers" that can end a relationship. For instance, no matter how much personal growth or healing you get, if you and your partner clearly differ over the choice of having children, the relationship will not survive.

A FOUNDATION FOR BUILDING LOVE

Shared vision is like a blueprint for a house. Only in this case, it's a conscious map for building a relationship. It gives you a foundation upon which you can be constructive. It guides your efforts to create something meaningful that will stand through time.

Many times, couples we see had already been exposed to many good techniques for building better communication, resolving conflict, and so forth. But techniques alone may not be sufficient and partners often forget to use them.

Techniques, no matter how great, are like knowing how to install a window, tile a countertop, or hook up electrical outlets. Alone, they do not tell you how to build a house. Vision is the blueprint for the home you want to live in. It sets the foundation upon which you build your home.

More accurately, though, shared vision involves you in a

process. It is not just the destination. It's the sign that points down a new road to be actively travelled.

When your vision is "Growth," it reminds and supports you to engage in a process of personal growth whenever challenges or upsets arise. It's not about getting to the end of the road. It's about how to take your very next step.

You are always at a potential fork in the road, whenever upsets occur. You can go down the Hole or toward a positive vision. A consciously shared vision supports you to move in the direction you truly want to travel as soulmates.

Next we look at specific agreements partners can make that will support their shared vision. We will expand on the shared vision of "Growth" to demonstrate this.

EXPANDING THE VISION OF "GROWTH"

Growth is an important element to include in a shared vision. We recommend that you seriously consider adopting it in your own vision. Who would claim to have no lingering wounds or sensitivities from the past? Who wouldn't benefit from expanding beyond unconscious and limiting patterns?

We also recommend that couples make their shared vision real by writing a contract of new agreements. We will see how one couple, David and Lisa, created such a contract to support their shared vision of "Growth." As we discuss their process, consider which agreements you would include.

The first part of their contract was to acknowledge that they each carried baggage from the past into the relationship. This was a commitment to their mutual willingness to claim and own their past baggage.

1. BOTH PARTNERS ADMIT THEY HAVE:

- Sensitivities
- Limited clarity
- Room to improve communication
- Differences, and that's okay
- Emotional wounds from the past
- Unrealized parts of self

David and Lisa started by admitting they each did, in fact, have sensitivities, limits, wounds, fears and old patterns. Each admitted that there were areas where they could grow and become more whole. They acknowledged they were different in some ways, and each said that was okay.

This agreement made it safer for them to claim baggage with each other, which was a vital part of their growth. They realized they were in partnership around personal growth and that each, in their own way, had to grow.

This led them to the next part of their contract, where they made an agreement that neither one of them was "right" or the other "wrong."

2. AGREE NO ONE IS "RIGHT"

- Move beyond blame & name-calling
- There's no identified "problem" person
- It's a "no-fault" partnership

Essentially, both David and Lisa agreed to move beyond judging or blaming each other, as a matter of first principle.

This didn't mean that they never reverted to pointing the finger again. It was, however, a formal statement that each of them recognized that judging and blaming were destructive. Saying this helped them see when they were doing it—and to stop doing it.

They also agreed that there would not be an identified problem person in the relationship. They embraced the fact that relating is like dancing, and that both partners were fully participating in whatever was happening.

In this sense, they adopted a "no-fault" partnership. Why wait for a no-fault divorce, when you can have a no-fault relationship? When you take away blame, you can more easily find the path to growth and happiness.

Next, David and Lisa explored mutual growth goals—of healing old wounds, expanding beyond their current limits, and finding greater personal wholeness.

3. JOIN IN THE MUTUAL GOALS OF:
- Healing old wounds
- Expanding beyond old limits
- Finding greater wholeness

The way both David and Lisa spelled out "Growth" came to include some of the other common words couples use for shared visions. "Healing" applied to old wounds. "Wholeness" applied to areas that frequently gave rise to conflict.

It turned out that many of their conflicts arose from differences between them in the emotional arena. David was quite comfortable feeling and expressing anger. He was from a family where members would raise their voices in anger, yet still knew they loved and cared for each other.

Lisa had a different background, and she had vowed at an early age to avoid anger at all costs because it caused so much pain. She typically would grow silent and distant around a show of anger, or anything that might cause it, and would also tend to suppress her own anger.

In the relationship, anger had become a trigger of upset, judgment and blame. David was triggered by Lisa's distancing when he was upset. He also was concerned with her failure to express anger. At the same time, Lisa judged David to be "wrong" for showing anger, and felt a lot of old pain when he expressed it.

Interestingly enough, when it came to another emotion, that of sadness, the situation was reversed. Although Lisa couldn't tolerate or feel anger, she was easily able to feel and express sadness. David, on the other hand, was trained to believe it less than manly to express sadness. He had learned to deny this human emotion within himself.

4. FOR EMOTIONAL GROWTH:

- All feelings are okay to feel
  (anger - hurt - sadness - fear)
- But NOT all ways of expressing
  these feelings are okay
- Make agreements about ways
  to express feelings

Eventually, they saw this pattern of emotional gridlock.

Their shared vision included "Wholeness" and they spelled out supporting agreements in the emotional arena.

They agreed that all feelings were okay. That meant that anger and sadness are both okay. They agreed that a whole person would be able to feel and express both emotions.

If anger is "red" and sadness is "blue" then they were, in effect, saying that a part of their personal growth is getting access to the complete spectrum, to have all the colors included in their emotional rainbows.

David and Lisa both admitted being cut off from a vital part of their own spectrum. Each acknowledged that many of their conflicts simply reflected their own personal lack of emotional wholeness. Thus both of them embraced the value of allowing all feelings to be okay.

In saying all feelings are okay to feel, they were not saying that all ways of expressing those feelings were okay. Lisa agreed that feeling angry was okay—but behaviors like touching each other in angry ways like pushing, grabbing or hitting certainly was not. And throwing things was not okay. David said that feeling sad was okay, but waking the other person up at two in the morning to try to resolve it was not.

They spent some time discussing other situations where anger or sadness might come up—and what behaviors would be okay or not okay in each case. Lisa suggested alternative ways David could express his anger that would work better for her. He told her ways to ask for his support when she was feeling sad. They also stated their support of one another in growing emotionally more whole.

The last part of their agreement explored ways to work with upsets and challenges as they came up.

5. AGREE TO EXPLORE NEW ROADS WHEN FACING UPSETS & CHALLENGES:

- Use upsets as material for growth
- Have a "Stop!" agreement
- Adopt a process to heal old wounds and transform negative emotions
- Get support from a third party

Here, David and Lisa agree to use anything upsetting or challenging that comes up as material for growth. They pledge to explore new strategies and do whatever it takes to face and move through challenges. To back this up, they made specific agreements for what they will do.

One was a "Stop!" agreement, which we'll present to you in the next chapter. They also adopted a powerful process for healing old wounds and transforming negative emotions, which they used whenever big upsets arose. We will present this later. Finally, they agreed to use third party help whenever they got stuck and could not work things out themselves.

When we first saw them, David and Lisa were on the verge of splitting up. Their patterns, especially the emotional gridlock, created a great deal of pain and suffering. As a couple, they spent a lot of time in the Hole. They had no idea that there was any other road they could take.

Committing to the shared vision of "Growth" was a dramatic turning point in David and Lisa's love life. The positive changes they made resembled other couples we have worked with, who had the same vision. Over the years, we have witnessed results that often seem miraculous.

RESULTS OF SHARED VISION "GROWTH"

- Partners embrace upset feelings
- Emotional learning happens
- Ownership of feelings
- Less blaming the other person
- Less acting out of emotions
- Less destructive communication
- Reduced influence of past 95% factor
- Past wounds & resentments healed
- Relationship is kept clear
- Feelings operate on the 5% level as balanced and appropriate signals in the present

As couples travel down the new road of "Growth," challenges are more easily faced. Upset is no longer a signal that it's time to retreat or attack, no longer a reason to think the relationship is bad or the other person is wrong. Instead, partners start to embrace challenges as opportunities for personal growth.

This enables emotional learning to happen. Partners learn to own their feelings, instead of blaming the other person or acting out. The 95% factor decreases as past wounds are healed. Old patterns are dropped.

The relationship is cleared of built up resentments and emotional gridlock—and it stays clear. Feelings operate more on what we call the "5% level" which is before the 95% factor kicks in. The 5% level is where feelings are appropriate to events in the present rather than being contaminated or turbo-boosted by the past.

Operating on the 5% level, partners can express and respond to each other constructively. Communicating on the 5% level works. You can successfully negotiate wants and needs, and find mutually satisfying solutions to challenges.

Once you have committed yourself to a shared vision, you have a clear motivation to operate on the 5% level and not fall into the 95%. You become motivated to use communication techniques that support your journey down a new road.

If you have any uncertainty at this point as to what your vision is, we strongly recommend that you commit to the following vision:

"Healing"—"Balance"—"Wholeness" & "Personal Growth"

Take some time now and expand your vision into a contract of specific new agreements. If you are in a relationship, and your partner is willing, do this together.

If your partner is not willing—they may need time—then do this for yourself as a personal vision. It takes at least one partner to change the dynamics of a relationship. Do this now whether or not your partner is ready to join you.

If you are single, do this as a personal vision. This will change your life. You can also do this with a close friend, family member or any meaningful relationship.

Next, we will explore new strategies and communication techniques that help you travel on a new road—the road defined by your new vision.

CHAPTER SIX

COMMUNICATING LIKE SOULMATES

"Experience is not what happens to you. It is what you do with what happens to you." —ALDOUS HUXLEY

The previous chapter was about the power of shared vision in a relationship. Shared vision includes how you see and understand what is happening, especially during times of challenge or upset. It taps into your highest power to view such times as an opportunity to move in a positive direction rather than going to the Hole.

We pointed out that a shared vision is one of the two "differences that make a difference" in relating. The other such difference is the road you take. This is the behavioral component that complements your vision.

Building on the story of the five stages of relationship, this section will give you tools and techniques for how to take a different, more positive road together.

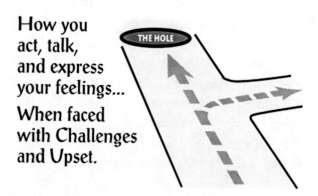

How you act, talk, and express your feelings...

When faced with Challenges and Upset.

THE HOLE

The road you take is how you act, talk and express your feelings, especially when faced with challenges or upset. Recall the road that most couples do take when faced with upsets. It's the familiar downward spiral. Partners go around and around the vicious circle until they land in the Hole.

FAMILIAR ROAD
with Challenges and Upset

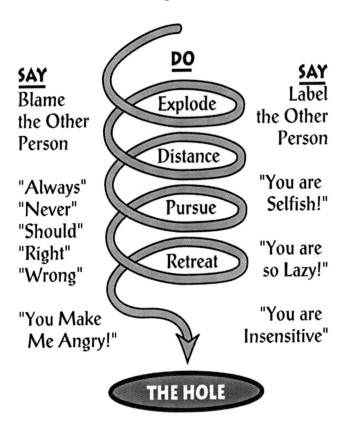

SAY
Blame
the Other
Person

"Always"
"Never"
"Should"
"Right"
"Wrong"

"You Make
Me Angry!"

DO
Explode
Distance
Pursue
Retreat

SAY
Label
the Other
Person

"You are
Selfish!"

"You are
so Lazy!"

"You are
Insensitive"

THE HOLE

We have already discussed this road in depth, all the way down to the bottom of the Hole. Faced with challenges or upsets, partners become reactive. Their 95% factor kicks in from the past and turbo-charges emotions to a level where it is impossible to interact in a constructive way.

Instead of getting to a positive resolution, partners dig themselves in deeper. They blame and criticize one another, each seeing the other person as the cause of the upset. They get defensive, distance or stonewall. At 95% a full fight or flight reaction is operating.

In the Hole, there is no possibility of a mutual solution. Each wants to be "right" and therefore the other must be "wrong." Someone has to "lose" and nobody feels accepted. It is clear from the outside that partners are only damaging their love.

FIRST STEP TO A DIFFERENT ROAD
with Challenges and Upset

The first step to a different road when facing challenges and upsets is to recognize the damaging effect of the 95% factor. See the Hole, don't pretend it's not there, and don't let yourself be tempted to jump into it!

Trying to solve anything in the Hole is like trying to balance spinning plates when you are fall-over drunk. Emotional reactions alter the chemistry of the body and mind just as surely as any strong intoxicant.

Talking from the Hole, partners end up saying things they later regret and perhaps didn't even mean. The damage from the discussion about the problem can be far worse than the problem itself. Partners misunderstand one another more often than not, and further inflame the issue.

The attempt to solve things once the 95% factor has kicked in is like trying to put a fire out by throwing gasoline on it. It is vital for partners to recognize and admit they do more damage than good when they go down the road to the Hole. Then agree to do something different!

STOP THE MADNESS

We ask couples, "Can you remember one time when you went into the Hole and resolved an issue in a mutually satisfactory way?"

Usually there is silence...

Then we ask, "Can you name times when you went into the Hole and things just continued to get worse?" There is no shortage of reports where upsets escalated beyond control. Things said were taken the wrong way and there didn't seem to be any way to get through and be understood. Partners were left in an emotionally exhausted state, with even more to deal with than the original problem.

When we go into the Hole, we are being dominated by issues and emotions from the past. What we are trying to resolve has less to do with a current partner than it does with deep seated old wounds. We are most likely trying to resolve old wounds with parents or others from our past.

Yet the way we project that onto our partner now will only hurt our current love. Are you convinced yet that there is absolutely nothing that will be solved inside the Hole? Do you want to travel on a different road? If so, read on...

THE STOP TECHNIQUE

To travel on a new road, you must stop moving toward the Hole. This is the very first step. You need to take this step before you can begin to go in a new direction.

Let's say you find, unexpectedly, that you are involved in a situation where one or both of you are getting upset. You may already be going around the Vicious Circle. Or you may be at the starting line, about to engage in a familiar trip to the Hole.

Someone has just said or done something, and the other person is getting upset. The "Stop Technique" is what will keep you out of the Hole.

① Says or Does

④Upset

②Upset

③ Says or Does

JUST SAY... "STOP !"

What you do is just say "Stop!" That's it. Perhaps you use another word, like "Time Out" or "Whoa!"

If this sounds too simple, you are right.

It is an unusual thing to do, and therefore it will not be as comfortable as continuing to head into the Hole. Incredibly, couples are more comfortable with the familiar escalation to crisis, than with an unusual act like saying "Stop!"

You and your partner need to set up a Stop Agreement for this technique to be effective. We discuss that below. You will also have to learn to say and hear the word "Stop!" in ways that avoid further triggering emotional reactions.

But the hardest thing will be to remember to do it.

Let's address the actual meaning of saying "Stop!"

INTENTION OF SAYING "STOP!"

"Stop!" = "I'm not resourceful enough right now to hear you..."

- Recognize you're headed for the Hole
- Ask for time out to get centered
- Say you'll return to the topic later
- You want to reach a positive result
- You want to honor your shared vision

Saying "Stop!" is the same as saying:

"I'm not resourceful enough right now to hear you. I'd like to return to this topic later. If we continue discussing it now, I am afraid I will only end up in the Hole."

"I would like some time out now in order to center myself.

Then I would like to follow up and return to this topic in a couple of hours... when I will be able to better hear and respond to what you are saying."

"I want to reach a positive result around this topic—one that is mutually satisfying and honors our shared vision of Personal Growth."

"Is it okay with you if we continue this in two hours?"

Your shared vision may be different than "Growth." You may need more time before getting back to discuss the topic. Maybe you'll need to take a break—be alone and center yourself. At other times, you may only need to change the topic of conversation or be silent for a few minutes.

The important thing is to *stop* moving toward the Hole.

Saying "Stop!" is like putting a stop sign in front of the Hole. It says, "Wake up! We are about to go into the Hole if we keep going in the same direction."

Later on, when you are well practiced in the Stop Technique, you can learn to put up a detour sign or fluidly move around the Hole. You can even learn to take an abrupt right turn and travel down a new road.

The Stop Technique is the first step.

When I had recurrent back pain, my physical therapist told me, "If you want to start healing your back, you need to stop doing more damage to it. Stop lifting heavy objects!"

It seems pretty obvious now. And it worked. So does the Stop Technique. If you want to start truly resolving issues, you need to stop doing more damage to your love. Trying to resolve issues when you're in the Hole is the equivalent of lifting heavy objects when your back is already out.

MAKING A STOP AGREEMENT

To use the Stop Technique effectively, a couple needs to make a clear, specific agreement. This means writing up the agreement as a contract and signing it.

There is an example of what should be included in such a contract on the next page. The contract begins by stating its purpose—to stop engaging in behaviors that destroy your loving relationship and to act in a way that honors your shared vision.

The contract goes on to declare the specific behavioral agreements that support its purpose. These are all necessary for the Stop Technique to actually work.

Partnership Agreement

Purpose:
To Stop Destructive Behavior
To Honor Your Shared Vision

Terms to Arrange:

- Pick a Signal ("Stop" "Time-Out").
- It is Absolute. You Must Stop.
- Your job is to say "Stop" ASAP... as soon as you feel yourself react.
- Whoever says "Stop" proposes the time to come back together.
- Time Out = 1 hour - 24 hours.
- You must come back as Agreed.

There are six ingredients required to make a complete Stop Agreement. If you leave one of these out—or fail to observe it—the Stop Technique will not work.

1. You formally pick a verbal signal for "Stop!" This can be the word "Stop" or "Time Out" or anything else that will work for you. It should be short and clearly identifiable in any context.

2. You agree that when this verbal signal is given by either person, you *both* will immediately stop no matter what is happening. There needs to be no further explanation of why one of you has called a stop. No justification is required. You already understand the full meaning of the verbal signal and the intention behind using it. There is no debate. It is absolute. You stop!

3. It is your job to say "Stop!" as soon as possible — whenever you sense things are moving in the direction of the Hole. You must say it as soon as you realize *you* are starting to react. You don't wait or think, "We can solve this if I can just make my point" or "I can take a little more of this..." You say "Stop!" Hesitation to do this is the main failing point of most couples in using the Stop Technique. We will talk more about this point below.

4. Whoever says "Stop!" proposes the time and place to come back together in order to address the issue in a more resourceful way. It is then their primary duty to get centered in order to better hear the other partner.

5. Ideally, the time out period should be at least one hour, but not more than 24. You can agree to exceptions. Work within the schedules of each partner to find a time where you both are most likely to be resourceful.

If you use third party counseling or coaching, it may be better to take the issue to session. You might more easily resolve the issue and learn new communication skills at the same time.

In the beginning, some couples we work with declare several "Stop's" during the week and postpone resolution until they see us. They report that they continue to interact in loving ways in the meantime, feeling like a weight has been lifted off their backs.

6. You must come back as agreed. The Stop Technique is not a method for avoiding important issues. It's a way to stay resourceful and on the 5% level of feelings where you can still successfully negotiate wants and needs and find mutual resolution. It's a way to keep the heat of the 95% factor from kicking in, turbo-charging your emotional states and taking you into the Hole.

USE IT OR LOSE IT

Partners often hesitate or forget to say "Stop!" This is the main failing point we have seen. You've got to use it or you will lose it. By "losing it" we mean you'll fall in the Hole.

The story[4] of the four monks shows how easily we can be sidetracked from keeping an agreement to stop. The four agreed to meditate silently without speaking for two weeks. By nightfall on the first day, the candle began to flicker and then went out. The first monk said, "Oh, no! The candle is out." The second monk said, "Aren't we not suppose to talk?" The third monk said, "Why must you two break the silence?" The fourth monk laughed and said, "Ha! I'm the only one who didn't speak."

For it to work, you have to remember to keep the Stop Agreement. Some people may think that saying "Stop!" is an act of copping out or showing weakness. Others may be afraid they could insult their partner or further rock the boat. So they just "forget" to say it.

But saying "Stop!" is a gift to the relationship, and to each other. It stops an all too predictable journey to the Hole before more harm is done. It sets up an interval of time for you to get perspective and center yourselves, so that you can later address the issue and get a more positive result.

So, to repeat, it is your job to say "Stop!" as soon as you sense things are headed to the Hole. If you are operating on a 5% level of emotions, appropriate to what is going on here and now, you can still achieve a positive result. As soon as you hit 10% and rising, you are closing in on the Hole.

You may start to feel sensations in your body that tell you the discussion is more heated than the issue warrants. A tightness in your throat or stomach, perhaps. Say "Stop!" If you wait until you hit 25% or 50%, it's already too late. It takes only 10 seconds for the 95% factor to fully kick in. By then you are lost!

Say conflict arises over not keeping the house as clean as the other wants. Maybe it's about that pair of socks discovered on the living room floor. At 5%, you can negotiate and find a mutual solution. At 10%, you may start hearing the words "You always..." or "You never..." It's time to say "Stop!"

If you hesitate, hoping things will be different this time, you are just sitting in the back of the Relationship Bus letting the ghost of the past take the wheel and drive you to the only destination on its map: the Hole. Say "Stop!"

It is your job to say "Stop!" Remind each other to take time out and return to the topic later when you can be more centered. You both can do things differently and create for yourselves a better chance to get a positive result.

PRACTICE MAKES PERFECT

When nurses initially learn to do CPR, cardiopulmonary resuscitation, they practice doing it over and over again—on a dummy. This allows them to integrate the new behavior so that they can perform it later in the heat of emergency.

It would make no sense to start learning CPR directly on a patient in critical condition. Similarly, it makes no sense to try to integrate the Stop Technique into your behavior by waiting until things heat up before you use it.

We recommend practicing a "Mock Stop"—once a day for a month. This is where you say "Stop!" but you are not feeling upset. You are just practicing the technique, so that you can more easily do it later, under fire.

It's great if you can practice a Mock Stop at a time when it seems to fit a situation, before there is any emotional upset. But this really doesn't matter. Whether or not such perfect situations arise, it is important to practice it every day.

Since this is a *mutual* agreement, your partner will also be practicing, and this will help you adjust to hearing the word "Stop!" and then respecting it rather than getting upset.

In a Mock Stop, simply say your signal—"Stop!" "Time Out" or whatever you have chosen. Then follow it up with, "I need to take some time out here, to get more resourceful. Can we continue this topic in five minutes?" Then leave the room if possible, or at least be completely silent for a full five minutes. During that time, breathe and center yourself.

CONSIDER THE ALTERNATIVE

Many people tell us "I called a Stop, but I still felt very upset. So what's the point of saying Stop? It didn't get rid of my upset feelings."

We have one answer. Consider the alternative.

If you went further into the Hole, do you seriously think you would end up feeling less upset? Be honest. You are only going to get more and more upset—as you and your partner say more and more unresourceful things to each other.

The sooner you stop your march to the Hole, the less upset you will have, the less time it will take you to get resourceful, and the less damage you will have to try to undo.

Why don't we all realize this?

Because the Hole is very seductive and tricky.

The Hole says "Jump in here! This is the way to get rid of your upset feelings. Act them out! Blame your partner!"

But the Hole is lying to you. Has that ever been true? Even once, have you resolved something from inside the Hole?

So, sure, you will say "Stop!" and then you'll still have whatever upset emotions you are feeling in the moment. In the silence of a Stop, you may even be more aware of them.

But consider the alternative—creating even more upset feelings and more damage. One more step towards the Hole and you are creating an even worse situation.

Don't let the Hole trick you into thinking you can get rid of your upset if only you prove you are right, or yell loud enough, or dump your judgments onto your partner.

Consider the alternative to Stop—increasing damage.

Then do the wise thing and say "Stop!"

ALL STOPS ARE SELF-STOPS

The real secret to the Stop Technique is that all stops are actually *self-stops*. It is vital to see the true inner reason that you personally have for using the Stop Technique.

That reason is simply this:

<u>You</u> don't want to go to the Hole!

If you have read this far, you realize that going to the Hole is destructive to any relationship. But that's only half the story. The rest is just about you. *You* have more to lose.

Going to the Hole is destructive to your mental well-being and probably even your physical health. Each step you take towards the Hole sets you up for more inner suffering, more mental rumination, more replays of your inner movies, more tension in your body, more stress on your heart.

Going to the Hole makes you act and talk in ways you will personally regret. Each step you take towards the Hole lowers your personal self-esteem and stunts your personal growth.

When you stop yourself from taking just one more step towards the Hole, you make a conscious choice that supports your own personal growth.

So anytime you say use this technique, you are really saying "Stop!" to yourself—for yourself. Saying "Stop!" is a way of taking good care of yourself.

Whether or not your partner is ready to join you in a Stop, you still owe it to yourself to stop. Sometimes this may mean being silent unilaterally, or even leaving the room.

Ultimately, you are responsible to take care of yourself.

IN THE HEAT OF EMOTION

Aristotle said, "Anybody can get angry, that is easy. But to be angry to the right degree, and at the right time, and for the right purpose, and in the right way—that is not within everybody's power and is not easy."

Communicating anger is especially problematic for many relationships. One partner may be sensitive to this emotion— and may become quite hurt by it. But in general, unless both partners really enjoy yelling, the way in which anger gets expressed will be an important factor that can determine whether love builds—or decays.

Avoiding conflict is certainly not the solution. Research indicates that couples who avoid conflict are very prone to divorce. The strategy of avoidance results in them removing themselves further and further, until no love is left. Studies also indicate that couples who stay married have just as many fights as those who divorce. What differentiates the two is the skill level they bring to communicating.

Anger is a natural emotion and needs to be expressed—in a skillful way. Anger is an important signal that something is not working for us, that we are not getting our needs met, or that our boundaries are being crossed.

Sharing these signals with one another is as vital as using indicator lights when driving a car. Letting each other know what is going on, gives the other a chance to respond.

It is not the emotion of anger itself that damages love. The real issue is *how* it gets expressed, the specific actions and words that accompany the anger.

There is a story[6] about a little boy with a bad temper. His father gave him a bag of nails and told him that every time he lost his temper, to hammer a nail in the back fence. The first day the boy had driven 37 nails into the fence.

Then it gradually dwindled down. He discovered it was easier to hold his temper than to drive those nails into the fence. Finally the day came when the boy didn't lose his temper at all. He told his father about it and the father suggested that the boy now pull out one nail for each day that he was able to hold his temper.

The days passed and the young boy was finally able to tell his father that all the nails were gone. The father took his son by the hand and led him to the fence.

He said, "You have done well, my son, but look at the holes in the fence. The fence will never be the same. When you say things in anger, they leave scars like these. You can put a knife in a man and draw it out. It won't matter how many times you say 'I am sorry'—the wound is still there."

The Stop Technique is a tool that helps develop a level of skill in the expression of anger. It helps you to pull back from the brink of the Hole, to stop yourself from acting out the anger on automatic pilot.

When you take time out, it is your job to get centered and resourceful, so you can come back together and express your message with skill. After all, if it was important enough to blow up about, it's important enough to express well.

There are countless recommendations for how to work through anger during a time out—from writing about it to engaging in physical exercise. Some people benefit by just sitting for awhile, breathing, and feeling all the sensations in their belly. Find out and do what works for you.

YOUR JOB IS TO BE HEARD

No matter how you do it, your agreement is to get into a resourceful state before you come back to the issue. During your time out, spend awhile thinking about how you want to deliver your message to your partner.

A wise man[9] said: "Two monologs do not make a dialog."

The process of communicating involves two people. We can easily forget this. We usually see communication only from our own point of view. We know what we mean to say, and it's our partner's job to understand us. A grammarian fell into a well one day and had difficulty climbing up the slippery sides[6]. A little later, a Sufi chanced by and heard the man's cries for succor. In the casual language of everyday life, the Sufi offered aid.

The grammarian replied, "I would certainly appreciate your help. But by the way, you have committed an error in your speech," which the grammarian proceeded to specify.

"A good point," acknowledged the Sufi. "I had best go off awhile and try to improve my skills." And so he did, leaving the grammarian at the bottom of the well.

Here is an important fact about communication:

The Meaning of your communication is... the Response you get!

The real message the grammarian delivered was to tell the Sufi to leave—by insulting him. Remember, it is *your* job to get your intended message across. So figure out how to express yourself so that you will be heard.

Partners often pay attention to *what* they're trying to say, rather than to *how* they say it. Hence this rule:

If you do not get the Response you want... then Do Something Different!

The Golden Rule for soulmates, as always, applies.

A story[10] of another man in the hole is warranted. All the village was gathered around the empty well, trying to get this man out before the sun went down.

They were shouting, "Give me your hand!" But the man would not respond.

Meanwhile, a Sufi came by and noticed what was going on. He made his way through the crowd, to the edge of the hole, and looked down at the man.

"What is your profession, friend?" he asked.

"I am a tax collector," gasped the man.

"Well in that case," said the Sufi, "*take* my hand!"

The man immediately reached up, took the Sufi's hand, and was pulled to safety. The Sufi then turned to the crowd, saying, "Never ask a tax collector to *give* you anything!"

It is your job to notice whether your intended message is getting across to your partner. Notice their response. If it is not what you intended, then respect the importance of your intention—and change *how* you are communicating.

Recall how Sarah reacted when Michael tried to lighten things up by teasing. If he stayed true to his intention and applied the Golden Rule, then he might have said, "Wow! That really upset you. I'm sorry—that wasn't my intention. Do you want to talk about it?" Then he'd just listen.

RETURNING LATER TO THE SAME TOPIC
- State your shared vision
- Honor your vision
- Ask "How would I do this if I were already healed and whole?"
- Do things differently

When returning from a Time Out, start the discussion of a potentially charged topic by stating your shared vision. Say something like, "Our shared vision is 'Growth.' Let's keep in mind as we talk that we share the purpose of growth."

Remember your shared vision as you talk and listen to each other. In this example, make a little card with the word "Growth" written down on it. Then put that card out in clear view so both of you can see it.

How you sit or stand has an influence. If you directly face each other, it is a setup for a fight. You can avoid this by positioning yourselves side-by-side. If you have made a card as suggested above, then both of you could look towards it as the third point of a triangle. The card will remind you to honor your vision as you talk and listen.

Before any talking starts, take a moment in silence to go inside yourself and get in touch with your shared vision. Ask yourself, "How would I listen right now if I were already healed?" Before you talk, ask yourself, "How would I say this if I were already healed?"

Pay attention to the answers you get inside—they may guide you to do something more constructive. You may not feel comfortable doing it. But remember, discomfort is a sign that you are going down a new road!

Do things differently. Create new ways to talk together. There are several things you can do that might be different. Here is a partial list. Try these and make up others.

CREATE NEW WAYS TO TALK TOGETHER
- One Talker - One Listener technique
- Short durations (5 minutes)
- Create safety (vs. fixing things)
- Really listen (vs. figuring it out)
- Be resourceful (vs. solving it)
- Claim your baggage
- Do an emotional transformation process
- Get support from a third party
- "Stop!" if what you do doesn't work... and then Do Something Different!

ONE TALKER - ONE LISTENER. Let one person talk and the other just listens. This is "doing something different" from the usual back and forth talking, where neither partner ever feels they are heard. We will present a lot more about the One Talker - One Listener Technique.

SHORT DURATIONS. The goal is to stay constructive, so make your discussion brief. Limit it to five minutes. Only one person talks for that period of time. Stop and return to the topic again in an hour or two, when the other person gets their five minutes to talk.

CREATE SAFETY. Keep your focus on how to create more safety for both partners in talking and listening. Instead of just having your "eye on the prize" of getting your point across, keep looking at whether what you are doing is creating safety.

Talk about how to create more safety in dealing with issues. Sometime, when you are not in the Hole, ask each other, "What would create more safety for you when we discuss charged topics?"

REALLY LISTEN. Practice the art of really listening. You know you are listening when your mind is quiet, like a calm lake. No ripples. No thinking what you should say in return. Just breathe and be silent, inside as well as outside.

This is a vital skill. Without it, you have little chance of succeeding in love. With it, you are empowered to deal with a wide range of challenges in personal and professional relationships. Take every opportunity to practice it.

BE RESOURCEFUL. Couples often get lost trying to solve an issue. They have their "eye on the prize" of resolving the single matter in front of them. But remember, each challenge is an opportunity to develop skills and resources. These will help you better meet every future challenge.

So keep your eye on the real prize, not just the topic of the day. Ask yourself, "What positive resources would help me here?" Perhaps that would be "confidence" or, say, "compassion." Then before you start talking or listening, spend five minutes finding this resource within yourself. Remember other times you felt that way. Connect to that feeling now, and keep in touch with it throughout your discussion of the topic.

CLAIM BAGGAGE. Every time you discuss a charged issue, it is a good opportunity to go to the Baggage Claim Area. We covered this extensively in prior chapters. We will follow with more examples.

EMOTIONAL TRANSFORMATION. Go beyond the current topic and heal old wounds. Use the currently charged feelings and engage in a process to transform your negative emotions. We present such a process in the next chapter.

GET THIRD PARTY HELP. If you don't seem to be able to go anywhere but the Hole, seek guidance from a third party. It may seem impossible at times to be constructive with a charged topic. A third party can see options and positive choices that neither of you can see when you are traveling to the Hole.

The third party can be a wise friend or a professional counselor. If you truly wish to improve your resources and communication skills, remember the value of third party guidance. There is no quicker way to learn to do something different than getting a view of how someone else, who is not charged up by your topic, would address the challenge.

STOP AGAIN. If what you are doing does not work, and you are moving to the Hole again, go ahead and say "Stop!" This is a fundamental skill. The Stop Agreement is always in effect, even when you are returning to the topic later.

ONE TALKER - ONE LISTENER TECHNIQUE

- Listener is whoever said "Stop!"
- Listener sets when to come back
- Keep to a short duration (5 minutes)
- Start by stating your shared vision
- Don't switch roles for at least an hour

Now, we will present the One Talker - One Listener Technique in detail. Variations on this communication tool have been around for decades. It has been suggested by many relationship experts, counselors and therapists. It is well worth mastering.

This technique is truly "doing something different" from the usual back and forth talking, where neither partner feels heard. It stops that pattern cold. It gives each partner the chance to feel like they are really heard. When is the last time that happened to you?

We have found the following elements to be important in the One Talker - One Listener Technique:

1. The Listener is whoever said "Stop!" Remember, the full translation of "Stop!" is "Let's return to the topic later, when I'll be resourceful enough to hear you." So if you call time out, your job is to center yourself and come back and be the Listener at a later time.

2. The Listener sets the duration of how long the Talker has to say what they need to say. When you start using this technique, we suggest 5 minutes. Then it can get longer as you

both get more skillful in using the technique.

3. Start by stating your shared vision. Say something like, "Our shared vision and highest intention here is Growth."

4. When the time is up, don't switch roles for at least an hour. After the Talker finishes speaking for their 5 minutes— take an hour Time Out. Wait 60 minutes before the Listener becomes the next Talker, and speaks for their 5 minutes.

THE ROLE OF LISTENER: BE QUIET

- **Center yourself and breathe**
- **Silently hold your shared vision**
- **Don't be reactive, dodge all arrows**
- **Say "Stop!" again and reschedule if reacting**

The Listener's job is to hear what their partner says. They are silent on the inside and outside. So if you are the Listener, you need to develop these skills:

1. Pay attention to your breath. Keep breathing. Be centered. Feel your feet on the floor, contacting the earth below. Just relax. There's nothing to think, say or do here.

2. Silently hold your shared vision. If it is "Growth," then sense how growth is happening right now as your partner speaks. Don't try to figure it out. Just see it that way. See an alternative version of you and your partner where you both are growing. Keep that image alive in your mind's eye.

3. If you feel yourself react, remember your breath and let go of the energy of reacting. Breathe it out. Pretend you are dodging arrows. What your partner says might seem like an arrow coming at you. Let it go right by. There's nothing you have to do about it. Don't grab onto the arrow. That is the same as jumping in front of it. Don't think of making your own point. A point is at the tip of an arrow, and it can only hurt you!

4. If you do grab onto an arrow and start to inflict it upon yourself, you may react instead of listening. That's a signal for you to say "Stop!" and reschedule for later, when you can just listen to and hear your partner.

Here's a story[4] of a great warrior that tells how to listen. Though quite old, he still was able to defeat any challenger. His reputation travelled far and wide throughout the land and many students gathered to study under him.

One day an infamous young warrior arrived at the village. He was determined to be the first man to defeat the great master. Along with his strength, he had an uncanny ability to spot and exploit any weakness in an opponent.

He would wait for his opponent to make the first move, thus revealing a weakness, and then would strike with merciless force and lightning speed. No one had ever lasted with him in a match beyond the first move.

Much against the advice of his concerned students, the old master gladly accepted the young warrior's challenge. As the two squared off for battle, the young warrior began to hurl insults at the old master. He threw dirt and spit in his face. For hours he verbally assaulted him with every curse and insult known to mankind. But the old warrior merely stood there motionless and calm. Finally, the young warrior exhausted himself. Knowing he was defeated, he left feeling shamed.

Somewhat disappointed that he did not fight the insolent youth, the students gathered around the old master and questioned him. "How could you endure such an indignity? How did you drive him away?"

"If someone comes to give you a gift and you do not receive it," the master replied, "to whom does the gift belong?"

WATCHING THE VOLCANO

As a Listener there's an inner image that might help you in staying centered. Imagine a volcano releasing its energy. You don't want to plug up a volcano. Just ask a geologist.

Likewise, it's not very productive to interfere when your partner is releasing their steam. Don't try to make sense of, fix, or change what your partner is saying—or feeling. Don't try to talk them out of it or take it on yourself. Don't correct their words or story.

Even with the most helpful of intentions, doing any of those things interfere with your partner's process. It's like putting a plug in the volcano. It won't work!

All you have to do is watch—and dodge whatever seems to be coming at you. There's really nothing else you *can* do. That is the wisdom of watching the volcano.

The anthropologist Gregory Bateson made the following observation[12]. He studied cultures and languages around the world. He observed that people are saying one of two things at all times, no matter what the topic or what the words. They are saying either that they feel reasonably content or that they are upset. The words and story doesn't matter.

When the volcano emits gas, fire, lava, smoke or ash—it is releasing pressures you don't want to block or let build up further. This is a natural process.

In relationship, as emotions are released, the presence of a partner who is truly listening can lead to a great inner healing. Trying to block this release, by not listening or otherwise interrupting your partner will only lead to bigger blowups down the road.

Encourage your partner to express all they need to release. It clears the way for better communication later. The wisdom is to stay centered and listen—and not be reactive yourself. So call a "Stop!" if you start to react.

The skills of being a good Listener are key to taking a new road and becoming a true soulmate.

THE ROLE OF TALKER: BE CONSTRUCTIVE

- "I" Statements: factual, non-debatable
  "You were an hour late. I felt hurt."
- Move beyond name-calling or blame
- Make requests for what works for you
- Claim your baggage—the 95% factor
  "What's coming up from my past is..."
  "This is like when I was young and..."
  "This is a familiar feeling for me..."

The Talker's job is to communicate in a way their partner can hear. This means being as constructive as possible under the circumstances, and honoring your shared vision.

Ideally, we would already know how to express ourselves in a constructive way. But the reality is that we don't. This is a skill that can be learned and refined. It is "doing something different" when talking about a charged topic. Awkward at first, it's a matter of practice.

A Talker's job is to practice these new skills:

1. Make "I" Statements. An "I" Statement includes only factual, non-debatable items. A typical example is "You were an hour late. I felt hurt." All facts. Nothing can be debated by either party. This simple way of talking works better than the kind of "You" Statements we usually make.

2. Move beyond judgment and blame. Don't just dump your feelings on your partner in the form of name-calling or

blaming them for how you feel. That will only inspire them to react and go to the Hole.

3. Make a specific request about what might work better for you in the future. For instance, "You were an hour late. I felt hurt. In the future, it would work better for me if you could call me whenever you know that you might be more than ten minutes late."

4. Go to the Baggage Claim Area. Use the upset feelings that are coming up to direct you towards the 95% factor that is kicking in. This creates better understanding and healing.

MAKING "I" STATEMENTS

An "I" Statement includes only factual, non-debatable items. Most often this is a factual description of the specific behavior of your partner and the specific emotion you felt.
Here are some examples:

- "You were 60 minutes late. I felt hurt."
- "You told them my secret. I feel sad."
- "You didn't thank me for cooking. I feel upset."
- "You didn't wash dishes as agreed. I feel angry."

Each behavior is specific and non-judgmental. Each feeling is an actual, specific feeling like "anger" "hurt" "sad" "upset" or "afraid." You specify what they said or did and the emotion that you felt. This is information, not an attack or a judgment.

Making an "I" Statement is not easy. We are blind to the amount of interpretation and judgment we routinely insert in talking. Here are the above examples—contaminated with added judgments, and turned into "You" Statements:

- "You were inconsiderately late!"
- "You have such a big mouth!"
- "You take me for granted!"
- "You're so irresponsible, just like a little boy!"

When someone hears such judgments, they tend to get defensive. A judgement is an opinion—an interpretation of the facts—and it invites debate. By not sticking to factual, non-debatable "I" Statements, you are likely to trigger the Listener and push them into the Hole.

In driving, that maneuver is called a "You-Turn."

The second part of the "I" Statement, where you state the feeling, is also routinely contaminated. People think a proper statement is anything that starts with the words "I feel..." Wrong! Here are the second parts of the examples, made bogus by judgment:

- "I feel you are rude and inconsiderate!"
- "I feel betrayed!"
- "I feel unappreciated!"
- "I feel a lack of sincerity here!"

These are not feelings at all. For instance, "You are rude" is a judgment of the other person. It is not an emotion. Neither is "unappreciated!" It's a guess about what the other person is thinking about you.

Here's how to form the second part of the "I" Statement. Start with "I feel..." or "I felt..." Then choose from the following words: "angry" "hurt" "sad" "upset" or "afraid."

Another mistake people make with "I" Statements is to imply their partner "causes" what they feel. Examples:

- "You made me angry when you were late!"
- "You were late and that made me angry!"

This is just another form of blame. It only leads both partners deep into the Hole.

MAKING A SPECIFIC REQUEST

Another type of "I" Statement is to make a specific request to your partner for a behavior in the future. State the specific action you would like your partner to consider. Know that you are making a request, and they have the right to say no.

A request can be a followup to the "I" Statement above, or it can be made entirely on its own. Here are examples that would build upon the four statements that started the last section. They all start with the words, "It would work better for me if you..."

- "...call me if you are going to be late."
- "...keep my secrets totally to yourself."
- "...say 'Thanks' if I do the cooking."
- "...honor your agreement and wash the dishes."

A request can be more than just a followup sentence tacked onto an "I" Statement. It can be an entire statement in itself. The request need be the only message delivered.

Any of the examples above could be part of a direct request. Start with the words, "I have a request. Please..." then make the request, "...call me if you are going to be late." Keep it short, simple and non-judgmental.

Just as with "I" Statements, you contaminate a request by slipping a judgment into it. For instance, "I have a request. Please be more considerate in the future. Call me if you will be late." The middle sentence is name calling. Your partner may get defensive instead of hearing and responding to your real request.

You need to avoid unintentionally setting off another trip to the Hole. If your message or request is important enough for you to have strong feelings, then it deserves to be delivered in a way your partner can hear it and be able to respond to it. As Talker, the delivery is your job.

THE REAL CHALLENGE IS TO DEVELOP YOUR SKILLS

Most of us get caught up in the *story* of what "makes" us upset. We try to communicate this to our partner, in hopes that they will hear us, understand and respond.

Unfortunately, we don't pay as close attention to *how* we are communicating our important message. Sometimes we resemble the grammarian in the hole who corrected the Sufi's syntax. We are like that when we just want to get the facts right, to correct our partner in some way. The usual result is that partners get defensive, we are not heard—and everyone ends up going to the Hole together.

Beyond any particular issue that may challenge you, the real challenge is to develop skills in delivering your message. Otherwise you are doomed to keep trying to work things out in the same old way, and end up in the same old place.

As Talker, give as much attention to *how* you express yourself, as you give to the content of the storyline of the day. Keep free of judgment or blame. Use short sentences and talk about specific actions or feelings. Make specific requests. Move on from there to explore the opportunity for personal growth or healing that can come of the situation.

As Listener, give as much attention to how resourceful and present you can be, as you give to the words in the storyline. Do not fall for judgments or try to change your partner's ideas or feelings. Just listen and do nothing.

No matter what the current storyline, the real challenge in relationship is to learn to do something different, to develop new skills and to travel on a new road together.

MOVING ON TO CLAIM BAGGAGE

One of the best ways to verbally begin to travel on a new road is to consciously recollect the past and realize how it is affecting your emotional reactions in the present.

It can be powerful to explore this information with your partner as a part of discussing any current issue. It is a natural followup to making "I" Statements and requests.

We call this going to the Baggage Claim Area. It defuses a situation and helps you make better sense of all the feelings that are coming up.

By linking charged feelings you have now to events that happened to you in the past, you can discover and heal old wounds. In the short run, it may seem unnecessary and very difficult to do this. But in the long run, it will lead you to share a greater understanding with your partner and can reduce the amount of suffering you encounter.

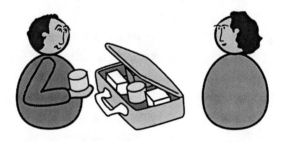

Here are some ways to begin talking about the past factor of your present feelings:

- "What's coming up for me from my past is..."
- "This is like when I was young and..."
- "This is a familiar feeling. It reminds me of when..."

Here is how that might sound. "You were late. I felt hurt. It reminded me of when I was young and my father would promise to pick me up after school and then be an hour late... or even forget to pick me up..."

Tell your partner the whole story of the past. Share what adds in to your upset today. "It led me to think he just didn't care... and I felt a sense of being abandoned. This seems to come up now for me when someone is late..."

You might even decide how to refer to this sensitivity. Maybe call it "my abandonment thing." This will help both of you to identify it in the future and not mistake the feelings that are coming up as just about the present topic.

Understanding each other's past baggage and 95% factors can help couples do things differently. Partners who live by a shared vision can better respect each others' sensitivities. They may change how they act and communicate with each other.

Informed partners can also focus better on healing the effects of past wounds. This is the road we will discuss next. It goes entirely beyond the verbal level of Talker and Listener discussed in the communication techniques above—and is a powerful path to transformation and personal growth...

CHAPTER SEVEN

MOVING BEYOND
THE TALK

*"You must be the change you wish
to see in the world."* —GANDHI

Recall for a moment the typical response when couples face challenges and upsets in love. The usual scenario seems as if the partners are in a boat that is sinking—and they are debating with each other over one question:

Whose side of the boat has the Hole?

- **Looking only on the outside**
- **Focused only on the present**
- **Not seeing the 95% factor**

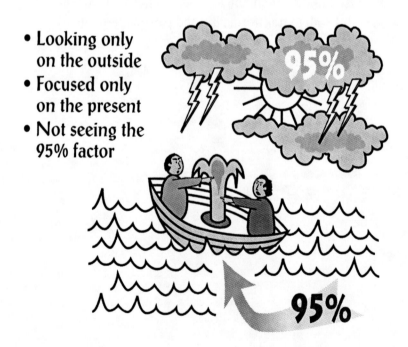

Not only is this a useless question, but it is the wrong question. It is based on the wrong assumptions. They are looking external to themselves for the Hole, when it is really something going on within each of them.

So a better question to ask is, "Where is all of this water coming from, anyway?" Is the water coming from outside— up from the ocean and down from the sky? Or is it coming from the inside?

Better yet to ask, "Is this water entirely from the present? Or is 95% of it streaming in from the past?" It is important to distinguish emotions based just on what is happening now from reactions that are being amplified by the 95% factor.

The best question of all is simply this:

What's coming up, asking for transformation?

Most of us can embrace the desire to transform and heal wounds from our past, to become more whole, and to expand beyond any negative limits set up by our past conditioning.

To do this we stop looking for solutions from our partner and we start to look within ourselves.

FOR TRANSFORMATION - LOOK INSIDE

Instead of looking outside for the source of the "Hole" in the boat, look inside to find the true source of the water.

Water is a traditional symbol for the emotions. Playing with this symbol a bit more, consider the following question about how you think of love and upset feelings.

Is the ideal soulmate relationship like a "boat" that is supposed to insulate you from having upset feelings—just as a boat would insulate you from the dangerous waters of the ocean? And if you do start feeling upset, do you conclude the Relation Ship has a hole in it that needs to be fixed?

Most of us do, in fact, think this way. Even though the majority may do so, it does not mean it is either accurate or useful. A majority once knew the earth was flat!

This way of thinking is about blaming our partners for what we feel. We tell a story about how they made us upset, in which we usually judge them and call them names.

Instead of looking outside for the "Hole" in the boat, it's more useful to look for the source of water inside ourselves. Water springs from within us. There is no hole in the boat. And the boat is not there to keep us from the water.

Here is a secret that only soulmates understand. It runs contrary to how most of us think—or even *want* to think—about love. Yet soulmates are willing to share and act on this little secret in times of upset.

Love brings up anything that is unlike itself.

What soulmates know is that deep, passionate love will naturally inspire us to move towards inner transformation, healing and wholeness. We glimpse this in the honeymoon, and start the real journey after that.

On the journey to wholeness we will encounter things within ourselves that are not yet healed or not quite whole. Old wounds will come up to bathe in the light of love. We will run up against past wounds, old sensitivities, emotional triggers and hot buttons. We will bump into limiting negative beliefs, old programming and old patterns.

Collectively, these wounds, sensitivities, triggers, hot buttons and inner limits make up what we have been calling the "95% factor" from the past.

This is what comes up in a loving relationship. This is the source of upset. While we may initially think it's an unwanted hole in the boat letting dangerous waters from the outside in, it is really something quite different.

The waters are within us. The light of love attracts these waters to rise. The waters arise with the intent of our finding transformation and wholeness—or whatever other word you use for it: healing, freedom, personal growth, balance, peace.

It is more accurate and more useful for couples to see the

emergence of upsets as a natural part of love. They will be empowered if they consciously hold a shared vision that understands and accepts this transformative process.

A shared vision is not some arbitrary thing that you try to attach to your relationship. It is a more accurate and useful way of seeing what is taking place. Shared vision embraces challenges and upsets as a part of love—sees these as a very positive and natural process.

A shared vision like "Growth" is naming something that is already deeply important within ourselves. To name it, is to stay conscious of it and to remember that transformation is a part of the loving journey. Remembering our personal vision keeps love afloat when the waters start to rise!

Transformation is a process of moving from the "Hole" to wholeness.

Think of transformation as the flowing of the inner waters towards the ocean of wholeness.

Instead of going to the Hole or thinking there's a hole in the boat, we can learn to just let the water flow through us. We don't have to block the water or build a defensive dam.

Most of us are so used to thinking of upset emotions as a hole in the boat, that the idea of transformation or wholeness may seem not only foreign, but unreachable.

It takes conscious effort to think in a new way and do something different. There are big rewards for making the effort to think differently about love and upset.

We encourage you to face the awkwardness, summon the courage, and make this effort. Remember, it takes conscious effort to move down a new road.

The road we are describing is real—and you can travel it. It is travelled by soulmates. It is a road where challenges and upsets are embraced, where partners heal and become more whole, and where love grows ever stronger as a result.

TRANSFORMATION - A DIFFERENT ROAD

It's an inner journey—a flow of transforming energy through the self—supported by your partnership in a shared vision.

Transformation is one word for a journey you can make as a part of being in an intimate relationship. Feel free to use a different word—one that matches your own personal values and vision. Whatever word you use for it, this journey involves the inner transformation of all that blocks you from fully experiencing and expressing love. We will continue to use the word transformation in reference to this inner shift.

Transformation can be experienced as a flow of energy through ourselves. The special energies of the honeymoon period are connected to this flow. Honeymoon energies are highly charged energies that are positive and magical.

The energies that flow in transformation are also highly charged. But we often label them negative and undesirable. So we block or stop the energy. We stay in our heads and become very mental. We try to turn the energy into words.

What we do is tell a story about what's wrong, who is to blame for it, and why it's such a bad thing. Sometimes the story is an attempt to fix or repair things.

What is missing in story-telling is to directly experience the energy that corresponds to our emotions. Perhaps this is protective, because we don't think we can truly bear feeling the feelings. Or maybe we truly believe we can solve things on a verbal level.

Whatever the motivation, we end up keeping our focus *above* the neck, in our heads—which in essence, insulates us from the flow of the waters. Unfortunately, this insulation acts like a dam, blocking the flow of our energy.

So the emotional energy underlying our "problems" is never released or transformed. It tends to stick around, build up—even clog up our ability to feel much love after awhile. We keep having the same discussions, over and over again. Then we wonder why our issues never seem to resolve.

We don't resolve these issues because we don't transform the energies *below* our neck. These unresolved emotions add into our accumulated baggage, our 95% factor—which in turn increases how upset we will get in the future.

The solution is to move our focus into the body. When we directly work with the energy below the neck, we can move towards transformation and wholeness. We will now offer you a process for doing this, one that you can do with a partner.

FLOW THROUGH TRANSFORMATION

We call this process Flow Through Transformation because it feels like an flow of energy through the body, a flow that results in a sense of deep inner transformation.

Do a Flow Through if you want to transform—rather than talk about—emotional upset. This process can even heal old baggage carried around from the past, your 95% factor.

It is a process that allows partners to do something different and to transform their charged up energies—rather than going to the Hole or getting into a stuck space.

Flow Through is like One Talker - One Listener, in that each partner has a distinct role. But it is far less verbal, plus the roles are renamed. What we previously called Listener is now "Witness," and Talker is now called "Flow Through." We will discuss each role in detail.

This process can take 30 to 60 minutes in all. Most of the time, you will schedule it for a time and place that works for both partners.

Just as with One Talker - One Listener, couples will often be inspired to set up a Flow Through process when one person has called a "Stop!" At that time, it may occur to either partner to invite a transformation process rather than come back and just talk about the event.

Typical invitations may sound like the following:

"I'd like to do a Flow Through with this upset. Are you willing to Witness?"

"Are you interested in doing a Flow Through around your feelings? I'm willing to Witness."

"After you said 'Stop!' I realized my upset had more to do with old baggage than with what happened here. I'd like to schedule a Flow Through. Are you available to be Witness anytime in the next few days?"

We will now describe each role, starting with Witness:

THE ROLE OF WITNESS

- It's a choice
- Stay centered and breathe
- Hold your shared vision
- Ask about body sensations

The role of Witness is a *choice*, and a gift to your partner. You are called on to be skillful and resourceful. So your first job as Witness is to schedule the Flow Through at a time and place where you will be resourceful.

Witnessing allows your partner to move through feelings to their own natural completion. It supports them to release upset, and creates a context for transformation to happen.

To witness your partner is to be available, centered, and compassionate. It calls upon you to be nonjudgmental and noninterfering. This will be deeply appreciated.

Many of the skills of Listener are called for when you choose the role of Witness. Let's start by summarizing the major skills involved:

1. **STAY CENTERED.** As Witness, you are centered and quiet within yourself. You keep breathing. You are aware that your feet are in contact with the earth. You let go of any reactions that come up within yourself, and just stay present with your partner.

2. **HOLD YOUR SHARED VISION.** In your role as Witness, you hold your shared vision, and keep moving your own energies toward that vision. This adds in a specific energy on your part to support the context of transformation.

3. **ASK ABOUT SENSATIONS.** Unlike the role of Listener, here you get to speak a bit. You will ask your partner very simple questions about what is going on inside of them. These questions will be phrased in terms of the sensations they are aware of in their body. This helps them to focus on the Flow Through process. We will discuss all this in detail.

STAYING CENTERED

As a part of transformation, your partner may feel highly charged emotions. You know, those things we normally try to avoid! So your own reactions might kick in.

If your partner feels an emotion like anger, hurt, fear, or sadness, how do you typically respond? Do you withdraw, reason with them, or take on their feelings? Do you try to fix them or make them feel better? What if they seem to blame you for how they feel? Do you end up getting defensive?

None of this really works for transformation.

To be Witness, we move beyond whatever reactions we typically have. We need to put aside whatever keeps us from holding the clear vision and energy of transformation.

Examples are:

- **Feeling it's our fault**
- **Getting defensive**
- **Taking on our partner's feelings**
- **Wanting them to feel different**
- **Trying to fix them**
- **Pulling away from them**

Each of those reactions is a signal to breathe in fresh air, and breathe out whatever is coming up. The job of Witness is to stay clear and quiet within.

Take deep, regular breaths. Be sure to keep on breathing. Feel yourself solidly connected with the earth. Let your mind be quiet and still, like a tranquil lake.

If thoughts or judgments begin to surface, simply put them

aside, and bring your focus back to your partner. If you have an urge to take care of their feelings or if you start to feel emotions yourself, breathe deeply, let go, allow it to pass through you.

It's more important to stay clear, centered and available. If you cannot do this—take Time Out. Return to the process later. This is a major skill. It takes practice.

HOLDING THE VISION

As Witness, it's your job to hold sight of your shared vision. See your vision, and how it gives meaning to what you are doing together right now.

Do not make the mistake of taking anything your partner says personally. Instead, see your partner as simply releasing emotional energy through their words. Allow them to release that energy. Realize that they cannot be rational right now, and that what they say may not be accurate. This is part of the process.

It may help you to know that they are releasing energy from their past—feelings that have been locked up inside since childhood, a previous relationship, or earlier in your relationship. Wherever this energy is coming from, while it remains unreleased it affects both of you, building up power as long as it stays locked inside.

As Witness, see that, at long last, this may be a moment of great transformation. The best support you can give them in their transformation is to just let your partner feel whatever comes up. Trying to fix them or make them feel better only interrupts the transformation process.

Give them a rare gift that can really help them to heal, your absolute presence. Know that they themselves have the power to release and transform. Your presence is all that's needed to support them in moving through their darkness.

SEEING THE SUN RISE

It is helpful to practice the following visualization:
Imagine the sun above as you sit with your partner.

Even in the middle of the night, you know the sun still exists. It may be a dark hour emotionally, yet you know for sure the sun will rise again. There may be clouds covering it, even the rain of tears or anger, but the sun still exists.

Imagine a globe of golden sunlight filling your chest. Feel its warmth. Feel it expanding from your heart, sending its rays of light out to your partner.

Then start to imagine how they will appear when their own

sun finally rises fully within them! Even if they seem to be going through highly charged feelings, imagine in your mind's eye how they will look when their own sun rises inside of them.

See that golden globe filling their chest. Sense how it is connected with the golden warm sunlight that so easily keeps pouring out of your chest, like a cup that flows over, and keeps flowing without beginning or end.

ASKING ABOUT BODY SENSATIONS

As Witness, you can speak to your partner. You ask them basic questions about the sensations they have in their body. The intent of this is to support them to stay focused on their Flow Through process.

Body sensations are the building blocks of emotions. They are the elemental components of feelings. When we move our awareness to this elemental level, the energies of emotion become more free to flow and change.

When we focus on the whole emotion, we usually say something like, "I am upset and angry!" Then we usually jump to the next thing, which is to tell the reasons and story of why we are upset and angry. The feeling itself tends to get locked in, blocked from flowing or changing.

However, when we move our awareness to the elemental level of body sensations, we might say something like, "I have a knot in my stomach" and then focus on what is happening in our body. We may report, "It is really tight."

As we pay even closer attention on this level, we will notice new things and can experience a flow of energy within ourselves. In moving our focus to this deep level of inner awareness, deep transformation can occur.

When you are Witness, part of your job is to help your partner stay focused on the elemental level of body sensations. You are asking your partner to describe what is going on inside of them in a specific way. Pretend there is an object inside them and you are playing "20 Questions" to figure out what it is.

Here are some guidelines for how you ask questions:

- **Be curious**
- **Talk gently**
- **Go slowly**
- **Wait a minute between questions**
- **Every question need not be answered**

The following is a set of questions you can ask. The set of questions works as a cycle that is repeated many times. These questions are simple, and have only to do with what your partner is directly experiencing in their body.

THE QUESTIONS

At the start of each set of questions ask, "What sensation are you aware of in your body right now?"

If your partner is aware of more than one sensation, ask them to choose one they want to focus on—perhaps to focus on the strongest one.

Once they have chosen the sensation they want to focus on, you will ask about various properties of that sensation.

Go slowly. Give them at least 15 seconds to answer each question. This helps them slow down and get more fully in touch with their sensations. Some questions may not get an answer. That's okay—just move on to another question.

"What is the location of this sensation in your body?"
"How big is it?"
"Does it have a shape?"
"Do you notice its weight? Is it light or heavy?"
"Do you notice its temperature? Is it warm or cool?"
"Do you notice its density? Is it solid, fluid or gas?"
"Does it have any pressure with it?"
"Is it stationary or moving?"
If it is moving, ask, "Is it just moving back and forth—or in a specific direction?" and, "How fast is it moving?"
"What is the texture of its surface? Smooth or rough?"
"Is there any color associated with it?"

The final question in the set is:

"Are you willing to just sit with this awhile more?"

At this point, pause and allow your partner to just be in contact with their inner experience. Then when it feels right, go back ask the first question, "What sensation are you aware of in your body right now?"

Cycle through the entire set of questions again.

If in this next cycle your partner offers answers like, "It is in the same place" or "It's still the same," ask them to pretend you are asking them for the first time, and to give you a fresh description as if they are noticing it for the first time.

Keep cycling through the entire set of questions. In most cases, the sensations flow and change, and there comes a time when it seems right to finish the process. Overall, the process usually lasts anywhere from 20 to 40 minutes. You will get a sense when it reaches a conclusion.

Now we will describe the role of Flow Through:

THE ROLE OF FLOW THROUGH

- **Move beyond the story**
- **Experience body sensations**
- **Patiently embrace whatever sensations come up, as you would hold a child**
- **Report qualities and changes in: shape - size - pressure - temperature weight - texture - movement - color**

Most of us have difficulty with upset emotions. Some of us stuff or suppress such feelings. We may deny feeling anything at all. Others deal with upset by getting stuck in the story of what caused the upset. This story usually includes blame, criticism and other things that lead us to the Hole.

Consequently, upset feelings often end up getting stored in our bodies. We may carry them around for days, or even years. This can affect our health and well-being. It will also continue to affect our love and relationship.

It is important to overcome our resistance to embracing the so-called "negative"or "dark" emotions within us. They offer us immense value, and are well worth the discomfort we may initially have being with them. In connecting with these unwanted emotions, we connect with long banished parts of ourself.

Think about the lotus when you are afraid of the darkness inside of yourself—that which you normally avoid.

In Eastern culture, the lotus flower is thought to have the highest spiritual qualities—of clarity and enlightenment. When we see it, our hearts may be warmed with the feeling of, "Ah, such blissful peace!"

Consider the lotus flower a teacher on your journey to transformation and wholeness. Its roots sink deeply into a muddy, murky substance. It draws nourishment from this deep dark place, grows upward through water toward the sun, and blossoms in its radiant flower form—offering love and delight to all who gaze upon it.

Learn to embrace your inner world as the lotus plant embraces the mud below. This is the very material that is transformed into nourishment, healing, love and wholeness. Your embrace is what transforms it so.

The Flow Through process is a way of preventing and even unraveling our emotional gridlock. Instead of pushing away feelings or getting stuck in the story, we meet emotions in a fresh, new way that leads to transformation.

Think about the word "emotion" for a moment. E-Motion. "E" stands for Energy. "Energy in Motion."

Emotions are connected with the movement of energy through the body. We can block this flow of energy. In fact, we normally do so when we stuff our feelings or get stuck in our stories.

But we can also tap into the flow of emotions on the level of movement of energy. And this has the power to heal us and make us more whole. To start this energetic flow, we need to move beyond the story and into the body.

Let's start by summarizing the major skills involved in the process of Flow Through:

1. EXPERIENCE YOUR BODY SENSATIONS. In Flow Through, you are called on to focus on the exact sensations in your body right now. Get very specific and stay in the moment.

Sensations are the building blocks of emotions. They are the basic elements. Paying attention on this elemental level connects us with the flow of energy and transformation.

You start with whatever you are aware of in terms of body sensations. An example might be the feeling of tightness in one's stomach or throat. You might say, "I have a knot in my stomach" or a "lump in my throat."

2. EMBRACE WHATEVER COMES UP. Much of the time, we would prefer not to experience upset feelings—or the body sensations that correspond to them. This attitude can block our emotions from flowing, and hence they get stuck in our bodies—and psyches.

You will get a lot more from the role of Flow Through if you take a different attitude. Consider the following analogy when it comes to how to be with your feelings. Imagine that you have a six year old child. You love them very much and are an ideal parent. You are sitting inside the house reading, and they come in the front door. They are feeling upset in some way, due to something that happened to them outside. As that ideal parent, what would you do?

Choose among the following options for how you would greet this precious child. Would you:

- **Tell them to leave**
- **Send them to their room**
- **Tell them to go away 'til they feel okay**
- **Say they shouldn't feel that way**
- **Tell them to stop feeling that way**
- **Take on their feelings and start feeling the same way yourself**
- **Just embrace and hold them**

Most of us know in our hearts that ideally we would just embrace and hold that child with total love.

This is the way Flow Through asks you to greet the sensations that come up in your body. Don't "send them away" by not accepting them into your space. Just let them in and hold them in your awareness. Embrace the experience, as if it were a child you loved very much.

One key thing that can help is to breathe!

Embracing your inner feelings is an ultimate act of self-nurturing and self-love. It is a pathway to inner transformation and wholeness. It's an emotional skill that can transform and move a stuck relationship.

3. **REPORT THE QUALITIES AND CHANGES.** Flow Through is about staying connected with the movement of emotionally transformative energies. You do this by reporting

to your partner about the qualities of your body sensations.

The questions that your partner, as Witness, will ask are designed to fine-tune your attention to your body sensations. You will be asked to describe their basic qualities, and how these qualities change over time.

Here are the qualities of sensation:

- **Location**
- **Size**
- **Shape**
- **Weight**
- **Temperature**
- **Density**
- **Pressure**
- **Motion**
- **Texture**
- **Color**

Take your time and just notice whatever you notice for each question. There is no "right" answer. You may not be able to answer all the questions, and that's okay.

If you even get a sense of something, just go with it. The point is to connect to whatever is going on inside of you. Embrace it. Let it be alive in any form it takes.

If you get more specific images, report those. Some people get colorful images of shapes that can even become recognizable. It is your experience. The important thing is to accept it and move with it.

When your partner asks you the same questions, even if nothing seems to have changed, report your experience as if it were fresh and new. Avoid just saying something like "It's still the same."

SUSPENDING JUDGMENT

The Flow Through process allows us a different way of experiencing emotions: being present, breathing, and allowing them the time and space to flow through you. It is the process of moving beyond our normal stories or attempts to avoid feelings.

In moving beyond the mental level, to feel your feelings, you are called upon to continually suspend your judgment. For each thing that comes up, you are asked to simply accept it, as it is—and not want it to be different, or even to "mean" something. Simply allow experience to happen.

There is a Taoist story[4] of an old farmer who had worked for many years. One day his horse ran away. Upon hearing the news, his neighbors came to visit. "Such bad luck," they said sympathetically. "We'll see," the farmer replied.

The next morning the horse returned, bringing with it three other wild horses. "How wonderful," the neighbors exclaimed. "We'll see," replied the old man.

The following day, his son tried to ride one of the untamed horses, was thrown, and broke his leg. The neighbors again came to offer their sympathy on his misfortune. "We'll see," answered the farmer.

The day after, military officials came to the village to draft young men into the army. Seeing that the son's leg was broken, they passed him by. The neighbors congratulated the farmer on how well things had turned out. "We'll see," said the farmer.

In Flow Through, be like the farmer. Let sensations and emotions flow without trying to evaluate them. If something starts to come up, a part of you may want to label it, control it, or even keep it on hold if it appears to be "negative." But be like the old farmer and just say, "We'll see..."

A STREAM THAT FLOWS INTO TRANSFORMATION

Are there any feelings you hesitate to fully experience—like anger, hurt, sadness, fear, or grief? How do you try to avoid them? Have you ever noticed that when you don't let emotions flow through you, they tend to stick around?

A flowing stream can teach us much about how emotions naturally move. At times a stream runs shallow—at others, it runs deep. Sometimes it is gentle and slow, sometimes it reaches the intensity of white-water rapids. Yet a stream just keeps moving, even over rocks. Constantly flowing, it soon returns home to the ocean.

Flow Through encourages you to let your feelings flow. Feelings move like water. It's best to let them keep flowing—not to hold on, hold back, or try to stop midstream. If you open your heart and embrace feelings, all will be safe.

Confucius is said[5] to have been visiting a great waterfall, which fell a height of two hundred feet. Its foam reached fifteen miles away and not even fish could survive entering it. Yet Confucius saw an old man go in, and concluded he was suffering from troubles and wanted to end his life.

Miraculously, the old man came out alive and unharmed downstream, and with flowing hair went carolling along the bank. Confucius followed him and said, "I had thought, sir, you were a spirit, but now I see you are a man. Kindly tell me, how did you survive this water?"

"I have been going into these waters since I was a small boy. Plunging in with the whirl, I come out with the swirl. I accommodated myself to the water, not the water to me. Without thinking, I allow myself to be shaped by it. And so I am able to deal with it after this fashion."

FLOWING WITH THE STREAM

By not holding back, you won't keep feelings dammed up inside of you. If you don't push against them, they will remain free to move and flow like water, all the way through to transformation.

Do you recognize when you're pushing against a feeling? Can you tell when you are blocking an emotion or stuffing a feeling? Do you know when you're stuck in the story?

One indication is that you are trying to solve emotional problems through the mental realm. You become engaged in reasoning, judging, comparing, criticizing, blaming, labeling, justifying, ruminating, or rationalizing. But what you are not doing is simply feeling.

It's a bit like standing on the diving board, about to take the plunge. Experienced divers may engage in a brief mental preparation, like reviewing a short visualization of the dive they are about to perform. But beginners may get stuck in mental activity and never jump in.

We have all witnessed young people frozen on the edge of the board, unable to move any further. From our vantage point, we know they will be perfectly safe. Yet their fear of making the leap holds them back.

It requires a leap of faith to do Flow Through. We have been conditioned to fear many of our so-called negative emotions. We may literally believe we cannot survive if we allow ourselves to fully feel them.

So instead, we stand on the diving board, staying high and dry—in our heads, engaged in mental activities—as if that were actually going to resolve the emotional issue!

ENTERING THE WATER

Flow Through invites you to fully feel your emotions. Rather than staying in your mind, move your awareness down into your heart, chest, neck, and belly—to simply experience whatever you feel.

Meet it. Accept it. Breathe deeply. Embrace it. And just feel it. Without words. Without the need for it to vanish or go away. Feel it as if it's the only thing you have left to do in this lifetime.

If feelings are a stream, then dive in and immerse yourself entirely—and be thoroughly cleansed! You will be safe. You can learn to flow with the stream and enjoy water.

Remember the advice that the old man gave to Confucius about negotiating the rushing river falls, "Plunge in with the whirl—accommodate yourself to the waters, not the waters to you."

Remember the old farmer, and suspend the temptation to mentally evaluate whether you should take the plunge or not. Delay judging what you are beginning to feel. Just say, "We'll see..."

Remember the analogy of the young child, for whom you are the ideal parent. The child arrives upset. All you have to do is embrace the child. Apply the attitude of an ideal and loving parent to the emotions that arrive within yourself, and embrace their presence.

As you fully embrace your feelings, you will begin to appreciate their presence as friends—as long lost parts of yourself. You will be like the lotus, sinking your roots deeply into that dark substance that nurtures your soul.

As your sensations move and flow, one feeling may lead to a different, still deeper feeling. This may then lead to yet another, perhaps lighter, feeling.

In this way, like a stream, the energy of emotion travels along its natural path to transformation.

PARTNERING IN FLOW THROUGH

Letting feelings flow freely in the presence of a partner can support positive transformation—or it can lead to major turmoil! If your partner is willing and able to witness your feelings, it can be very healing indeed.

When they are so willing, and you are taking the role of Flow Through, beware of the tendency to stay in the mental arena. Beware of attaching any verbal labels, causes, reasons, or blame to what you feel.

Avoid going on and on about the story of what upsets you. Breathe in and out—and leave all the talk behind. The talk is only keeping you from the transformative experience of Flow Through, and potentially triggering your partner.

Simply experience your feelings, without a lot of words. If you can't do this, it would be better to stop, and come back to doing Flow Through again later.

When couples try to work out their problems by talking and talking, having the same discussion over and over again, there is probably an underlying emotional issue that is not ever being touched.

Flow Through is an entirely new road to travel. If you can do it with your partner, you will find a level of transformation and soulful connection that you never imagined possible.

DOING YOUR OWN FLOW THROUGH

Ultimately, the process of Flow Through is a gift that you give to yourself. It is not just for the sake of a relationship—nor is it merely a communication technique.

Flow Through is a practice that enables you to heal inner wounds and to become more whole yourself. By embracing the full inner spectrum of emotions, you unblock yourself and your ability to fully experience love.

With this in mind, start doing Flow Through now—even if you aren't yet in a love relationship, or even if your current mate isn't ready to do it with you.

SOLO FLOW THROUGH. You can do this practice alone, by just sitting down and being with what you feel. Breathe into the feelings and move your awareness below your neck. Parent the child within and get your own transformation.

TIME OUT FLOW THROUGH. Process your feelings during a Time Out. You will get more clear about what you truly want or need—and thus you will be more effective when you return to the topic later, with the other person.

PARTNERING WITH A FRIEND. Engage in this practice with a friend. Be there for one another in this very heartfelt way—and accompany each other in your transformation.

The next section summarizes the key messages presented throughout this book. You can use it as a checklist of things to remember for your journey of becoming soulmates.

CHAPTER EIGHT

STEPS TO DOING THE WALK

*"A journey of a thousand miles
starts in front of your feet."*—LAO TZU

Here are ten key factors that determine the quality of a relationship. These are essential ingredients in the recipe for becoming soulmates.

1. ACTIVE VERSUS PASSIVE

- **Is relationship a dance, or a bus ride?**
- **Does a great relationship just happen?**
- **Do you just meet your perfect soulmate... or do you learn how to be one?**

 **versus**

Do great relationships just happen, or are they created? Is love like a dance—or a ride on a bus? These questions focus on whether you are taking an active or passive stance in your relationship.

Many people just hope and yearn to meet their soulmate. This is a passive process. It depends on someone else being the

"Right" one for us. It will be this other person who determines the quality of our relationship—not us.

It's almost as if we have nothing to do with it. We are in the back of the bus. We comment on where the bus seems to be going. Who is driving the bus? That is the question.

We encourage you to focus on what it takes to be a soulmate. Being a soulmate is an active process. You play an proactive role. You are a partner in the dance. You can choose the steps you take, and pay conscious attention to how you are dancing.

2. CONSCIOUS SHARED VISION

Name the new road you want to travel

A shared vision is a powerful factor. It enables soulmates to see the road they want to travel together. If relationship is a bus, then you become the bus driver. Sharing a vision is the act of choosing which direction the bus is going, rather than passively waiting to see where it will go.

We encourage you to name the road you want to travel, whether that is healing, wholeness, balance, personal growth, inner peace, or any other word you want to use.

Go deep inside yourself and name what is truly meaningful for your own evolution as a soul. Discuss this with your partner and explore what your common vision is. Make this the foundation of why the two of you are together.

A shared vision is a pact between soulmates. It keeps you on track and guides you when times get rough. The vision is an active process that helps you find positive alternatives to going to the Hole. It empowers your partnership with deep purpose and spiritual meaning.

3. MAKE NEW AGREEMENTS

- **How can you create more safety?**
- **How will you work with upsets?**
- **How will you work with problems?**
- **How will you work with differences?**
- **How will you improve communication?**

Create agreements in line with your shared vision.

Discuss how you can create more safety in your relationship. Name what would assist you to have a greater sense of safety in being and sharing who you truly are. Ask your partner what would help them have a greater sense of safety right now.

Talk about and make new agreements for how to work with upset emotions, problems and differences. Discuss what you can do to communicate constructively, in new ways that get positive results.

Soulmates might agree to use whatever upsets come up as material for transformation. They might agree that problems point to places where each needs to expand. They might see differences between them as mirrors to parts of themselves they need to develop.

We encourage you to commit to communicating in ways that are constructive rather than destructive. Look closely at what helps the communication process feel safe and positive. Say what could bring a greater sense of safety into it for you, and ask your partner what would make it so for them.

4. IDENTIFY YOUR PATTERNS

Name what takes you to the Hole.

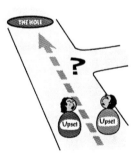

- Space vs. Connection
- Emotional Gridlock
- Labeling - Criticism
- Self-Defending
- Other-Blaming

Identify whatever patterns take you to the Hole. Look at how the dance between space and connection plays out in your relationship right now. Specifically name what goes on for you, and ask what goes on for your partner around closeness and distance.

Honestly assess any emotional gridlock that is happening in your relationship. Look at how anger, hurt or fear are triggered and expressed. Discuss whether there are feelings not being revealed, but stuffed or held onto by a partner.

Be very aware of any labeling, name-calling or criticism that occurs in your partnership. We encourage you to unravel such patterns, by facing and healing whatever emotions are behind the judgments or name-calling.

Another trap to watch out for is any self-defending that seems to come up in you or your partner. If you identify any place where you are acting defensively, then figure out what is needed so that you can do something different.

Look for any patterns in your relationship that involve blaming the other person, or making things their "fault." Discuss each pattern and recognize how it takes you to the Hole. Talk about what it costs your loving relationship.

5. CLAIM YOUR BAGGAGE

- **Own and name your part in it**
- **Share the info with your partner**

- **Sensitivities**
- **Triggers - Hot Buttons**
- **Past Wounds**
- **Emotional Patterns**
- **Family Conditioning**

An important factor in being a soulmate is to claim your own baggage. After you've identified a pattern that takes you and your partner to the Hole, look for the part you play in the dance.

Open up your baggage and share the contents with your partner. Specifically, name any old sensitivities, emotional triggers or hot buttons, past wounds, emotional patterns, or family conditioning that you carried into the relationship.

Admit what is yours and give it a name. Take turns and do this together. Share your information in the spirit of understanding and in the name of your shared vision. It takes courage, gentleness and a commitment to create a safe space.

Create the safety to open and share past baggage by agreeing to confidentiality and to never using anything against each other. Be respectful and compassionate. Act as a soulmate and open your heart to your partner's past.

6. CHECK YOUR LOVE COMPASS

- Stay awake... beware of the Hole
- Check every 10 seconds if near the Hole

N = New Road

S = Same Old...
S = STOP!

A primary factor in creating the relationship you truly want is to stay awake and conscious. Be aware of when you start to head in an unproductive or damaging direction. If you are near the Hole, get out your Love Compass.

Check your compass every 10 seconds. That's all the time it takes to go fully into the Hole. Before you say or do something, check and see if it will take you "N" or "S" - on a

New Road or down the Same Old road to the Hole.

If the compass is pointing "S" then do Something Different—or call a "Stop!"

It's up to you to stay awake. Partners dance to the Hole together, hand in hand. Watch each step you take. Make it the step of a soulmate, rather than a "Hole" mate.

7. DO SOMETHING DIFFERENT!

- **Do the opposite of what you normally do**
- **Change your emotional patterns**
- **Just listen - don't defend, blame or fix**
- **Move beyond the polarity polka**
- **Create better timing**

SOMETHING DIFFERENT

There's really only one rule you need to remember:

If what you are doing is not getting the results you truly want, then "Do Something Different!"

For instance, if you and your partner are getting upset over the dance between closeness and individual space, then do something different. Do what different? Look directly at the heart of the matter and do the very *opposite* of what you'd normally do. If you usually pursue connection and closeness, and your partner is seeking space—then just allow space. On the other hand, if you usually need your distance and space, then something different for you will be to stay present with your partner when you get that old urge to flee.

By doing something different you will change the pattern and expand yourself. This will be a challenge in itself, but you will be proud to meet it. You will ultimately be happy that you have developed new inner strengths and resources through doing something different.

More differences? Look for any problems you and your partner have with feelings. Do you have difficulties with anger, hurt or fear? Figure out how you can do something different. If you normally express yourself a lot, then hold back for awhile and contain your feelings. If you normally withhold your emotions, then express how you feel.

If you become defensive, blame your partner, or try to fix how they feel, then do something different. Instead of doing those things, just listen to your partner.

When you realize you are polarizing, do something else. Instead of fighting over your differences, learn from them. See where you can expand as a human and become more balanced and whole. Let your partner be your teacher.

Notice where timing differences create friction in relating and then learn new ways to dance together. If you differ in how fast you express emotions or how quickly you need to resolve problems, find a balance. If you have poor timing in the dance of closeness and distance—and it creates upset— seek a way to better balance your needs.

8. HAVE A CLEAR STOP AGREEMENT

- Stay awake
- Keep alert for upset
- Remember your job to say "Stop!"
- Do it

Soulmates are very motivated to stay out of the Hole. They are absolutely willing and able to stop themselves if they're moving toward the Hole. Soulmates value being constructive and adding positive energy to their relationship. They stay alert to where things are headed.

Have a clear Stop Agreement with your partner. Know what saying "Stop!" means—understand that it is a gift to your partnership and it supports your shared vision.

Remember to use "Stop!" Know that it is your job to say it whenever upset feelings are growing and you and your partner are headed toward the Hole.

Instead of letting things get worse, call for a "Time Out!" Take an hour or more so that you can do whatever you need to do in order to get centered. Honor your shared vision. Return later to discuss the topic when you are more resourceful.

Being able to make and keep a clear Stop Agreement is a minimal requirement for becoming soulmates. It shows you are willing to relate consciously and get beyond the habitual, automatic reactivity that destroys most relationships.

9. COME BACK TOGETHER DIFFERENTLY

- Act as if you are living your vision
- Consciously structure the way you talk
- Use One Talker - One Listener technique
- Schedule a Flow Through process
- Get support from a third party

In stopping a trip to the Hole, you take time out to get centered, process your own feelings—and get in touch with your inner resources. Later, you will come back to the topic or issue. The point is to come back together differently, to "Do Something Different!"

Come back as a proactive and true soulmate. Act and sound as if you are already living your shared vision.

Rather than being spontaneous in how you talk with each other, consciously structure the way you interact. Find ways to prevent yourselves from falling into patterns that take you to the Hole.

Practice the One Talker - One Listener technique. Eliminate the back and forth talking style that can so easily get out of hand. One person talks, the other just listens, for 5 to 10 minutes. Then, after at least an hour of silence on the topic— trade roles between Talker and Listener.

If you want to move towards healing the underlying emotional issues, move to the Baggage Claim Area. Locate, own and share with your partner your emotional baggage that is fueling the current challenge or upset.

Heal and transform your emotional energy by scheduling a Flow Through process with your partner. Learn to get beyond the story—and get in touch with the powerful energies that can flow through you and result in a deep inner transformation. Ask your partner to assist you in the role of Witness.

If all else fails and you keep going to the Hole, get third party support. Consult a wise friend or a counselor. Another person can see positive options that you and your partner will miss. Even soulmates get stuck. But they do not hesitate to use any means available to get unstuck.

10. TAKE THE LEAP!

- **Act according to your shared vision**
- **Ask "How would I do this if I were already healed and whole and ..."**
- **Do it even if you have fear or discomfort**

Taking a new road rather than going to the Hole would be the hands-down choice for most people. But to travel in an unfamiliar direction brings up fear and discomfort.

Most couples end up doing the familiar—and strangely more comfortable—thing, of just going to the Hole.

We encourage you to act as if you are already living your shared vision. Ask yourself, "How would I do this if I were already healed and whole?"

The point is to take new action—do that which is more in accordance with your vision.

Do this even if you are not comfortable. Discomfort is a sign you are traveling on a new road.

Take the leap!

SHARING YOUR NEW ROAD TOGETHER

You free up time and energy for:
- Creative activities and projects
- Making a contribution to the world
- Pleasure, health, exercise, just "being"
- Loving kindness in your relationship
- Being loved and feeling loved
- Words and acts that convey love
- Inner peace and strength from partnership
- Working together for common goals
- Modeling healthy relationship for others

When you share a new road together, you will move towards your shared vision. As you travel further along this road, the Hole becomes ever more distant.

You will spend less time being upset.

Couples that travel a new road find more energy for new and creative things. That could include activities or projects, making positive contributions to the world.

You will have far more time and energy for just being, for pleasure, for health and exercise, and for manifesting your dreams.

If you take up the challenge to *become* a soulmate, you are expanding the possibilities for loving kindness in your relationship. You will deeply experience loving—and being loved. You will share many acts and words that convey love to your partner.

There is a tremendous inner peace that comes from a loving partnership when you travel a new road. You know that you are working together for common goals, not just material but also spiritual. You feel a profound fulfillment.

As you travel along your new road, you model healthy relationship for children and everyone you meet—and you make the world a better place.

The following story[8] clearly states how to continue your journey from here, toward the relationship you want:

While waiting to pick a friend up at the airport, I had a life changing experience like you hear other people talk about—the kind that sneaks up on you unexpectedly.

Looking for my friend among the arriving passengers, I noticed a man coming toward me carrying two light bags. He stopped right next to me to greet his family. First he motioned to his youngest son, maybe six years old, as he laid down his bags. They gave each other a long, loving hug. As they separated enough to look in each other's face, I heard the father say, "It's so good to see you, son. I missed you so much!" His son smiled somewhat shyly, averted his eyes and replied softly, "Me, too, Dad!"

Then the man stood up, gazed in the eyes of his oldest son, maybe ten, and while cupping his son's face in his hands said, "You're already quite the young man. I love you very much!" They too hugged a most loving, tender hug.

While this was happening, a baby girl, perhaps one year old, was squirming excitedly in her mother's arms, never once taking her little eyes off the wonderful sight of her returning father. The man said, "Hi, baby girl!" as he gently took the child from her mother. He kissed her face all over and then held her close to his chest while rocking her from side to side. The little girl instantly relaxed and simply laid her head on his shoulder, motionless in pure contentment.

After several moments, he handed his daughter to his oldest son and declared, "I've saved the best for last," and proceeded to give his wife the longest, most passionate kiss I ever remember seeing. He gazed into her eyes for several seconds and then silently mouthed. "I love you so much!"

They stared at each other's eyes, beaming big smiles at one another, while holding both hands. For an instant they reminded me of newlyweds, but I knew by the age of their kids that they couldn't possibly be.

I puzzled about it for a moment then realized how totally engrossed I was in this display of love not more than an arm's length away from me. I suddenly felt uncomfortable, as if I was invading something sacred, but was amazed to hear myself ask, "Wow! How long have you been married?"

"Been together fourteen years total, married twelve of those," he replied, without breaking his gaze from his lovely wife's face. "Well, then, how long have you been away?" I asked the man as he finally turned and looked at me, still beaming his joyous smile. "Two whole days!" Two days? I was stunned. By the intensity of the greeting, I had assumed he'd been gone for at least several weeks—if not months.

I know my expression betrayed me, and I said almost offhandedly, "I hope my marriage is still that passionate after twelve years!" The man suddenly stopped smiling. He looked me straight in the eye, and with forcefulness that burned right into my soul, he told me something that left me a different person.

He told me, "Don't hope, friend.... Decide!"

Then he flashed me his wonderful smile again, shook my hand and said, "Goodbye." With that, he and his family turned and strode away together. I was still watching that exceptional man and his special family walk just out of sight when my friend came up to me and asked, "What'cha looking at?" Without hesitating, and with a curious sense of certainty, I replied, "My future!"

Don't hope.... Decide!

Goethe wrote that concerning all acts of initiative and creation there is one elementary truth: the moment one definitely commits oneself, then Providence moves too. All sorts of things occur to help one that would otherwise not have occurred. A whole stream of events issues from the decision raising in one's favor all manner of unforeseen incidents and meetings and material assistance which no one could have dreamed would have come their way. Whatever you can do, or dream you can do, do it. Boldness has genius, power and magic in it. Begin it now!

ACKNOWLEDGMENTS

Since meeting in 1989, we have been sharing a journey dedicated to transforming whatever blocks the full expression of love—in our own lives together, and in the lives of the couples we counsel and teach.

This book reflects what we have personally discovered on that journey. It also comes from the actual experiences of real people who have had the courage to transform their own limits—and to find what is only glimpsed at in the honeymoon. We would like to thank these people for sharing their stories and their lives with us. In writing this book, we have changed the names of these clients.

Among the many positive influences on our journey, we feel blessed to have experienced the writings and teachings of John Welwood, John Grinder, Milton Erickson, Gangagi, Gay and Kathlyn Hendricks, Ellen Pullyblank, Leona Tockey, Helen Palmer, and Charles and Caroline Muir.

We also want to thank our generous friends who read the manuscript, offering suggestions and support—Lisa Berg, Amara Rose, Arianna Husband and Richard Schoenbrun.

Additionally, we thank those friends who encouraged us along the way as we developed this material—Andrew Sears, Gordon Whiting, Ellen Weis, Timothy JohnPress, Jim Wood and John and Bonnie Gray.

Finally we would like to thank Ken Crittendon who not only offered encouragement, suggestions and support—but also drew the faces for our cartoon artwork.

NOTES

1. Unknown
2. Pulpit Helps
3. Unknown: www.cyberstory.com
4. Traditional story: collected by John Suler
5. Alan Watts: The Book
6. Unknown: www.inspirationalstories.com
7. Unknown: collected by Anthony de Mello
8. Unknown
9. Jeff Daly
10. Sufi story: collected by Idries Shah
11. Gregory Bateson: <u>Steps to an Ecology of Mind</u>

ABOUT THE AUTHORS

John Grey received a Ph.D. in psychology in 1975 from Stanford, where he taught and codirected a National Science Foundation sponsored research center. Since 1980 he has been in private practice and teaching workshops focused on communication, relationship and personal growth.

Bonney Grey, received a B.R.N. from the University of Wisconsin in 1979. In addition to a counseling practice, she presents communication trainings for medical professionals and psychotherapists, and leads women's groups that offer personal growth and relationship empowerment.

John and Bonney are passionate soulmates who spread the word that joyous and fulfilling love is possible on a long term basis. You *can* have the relationship of your dreams.

COACHING SERVICES

John and Bonney coach singles and couples throughout the country by phone. They also present workshops on conscious loving. And they offer a unique weekend retreat for couples to clarify and transform their relationships.

Information about these coaching services—as well as self-help tools—can be found on the internet at:

www. soulmateoracle. com

You can also contact the authors by email at:

lovegrowth@aol.com

LaVergne, TN USA
30 November 2009
165579LV00010B/47/A